EXPECT
A MIRACLE

EXPECT
A MIRACLE

A Mother's Tale of Brotherly Love,
Faith and the Race That
Changed a Family's Life

by
Jenny Long
with
Bob Der

Time Inc. Books
1271 Avenue of the Americas, 6th floor
New York, New York 10020

ISBN 10: 1-61893-128-8
ISBN 13: 978-1-61893-128-3
Library of Congress Control Number: 2015937594

DEDICATION

This book is dedicated to my boys. You're the best choices I ever made, and I love you more than anything. I will always be there for you. Someday, when you can't see me or feel my presence, know that I am beating in your hearts and blowing in the wind around you.

I also want to thank my dad: For giving me your best, no matter what. My mom: For 12 amazing years of love. I hope I am half the mother you were to me. All my friends and extended family: For supporting me when the times got rough—thank you for sticking by me and believing in me. And to my best friend (you know who you are): Thank you for accepting the whole package. It's not baggage—it's luggage, right?

Finally, to all the moms in the "special club": Hats off to each and every one of you, for all you do for the ones you love. The journey is unexpected, but so worth the effort.

—*Jenny Long, spring 2015*

To Liz: For your love and for trusting me with your heart. To James and Connor: You make me proud every day. To Mom and Dad: For a lifetime of encouragement and support. To Nancy and Peter: Without you, I wouldn't have Liz. And to my beloved uncle, James Joseph McCarty, who always wanted to be a writer.

—*Bob Der, spring 2015*

—contents—

FOREWORD

By LeBron James

From the moment I first heard the Long family's story, it touched me in a profound way. It was at the 2012 *Sports Illustrated* Sportsman of the Year ceremony, and I was there to accept the honor. But it wasn't me who deserved that distinction—it was Conner and Cayden Long.

To see the way Conner cares for his younger brother and the sacrifices he makes to bring him happiness left me speechless that night, and to this day I'm still at a loss for words when trying to describe what a true inspiration this family is to myself, my family and countless others.

In a word, the Long brothers are unbelievable. The fact that Conner competes in triathlons while bringing his younger brother along with him is unbelievable. And the way Cayden never loses hope, despite facing more obstacles than most of us will ever know, is unbelievable. Their strength, their passion for life and their dedication to each other are things we could all use a little more of in our lives.

As a father, you're always looking for ways to teach your kids certain lessons in life. I have to give Conner and Cayden a lot of credit for helping me show my kids how they should support and look out for each other. As Conner said that night at the *Sports Illustrated* ceremony, when they stick together, "we can always do anything," and I truly believe they will accomplish amazing things in life. They already have, even if at their young ages they don't realize it.

Conner and the entire Long family have left a lasting impression on me, and their story continues to be an inspiration for me in everything I do. They show us all what it means to persevere in the face of adversity. They are the real heroes.

THE FINISH LINE

I JUST WANT to see their faces.

I'm standing with hundreds of cheering parents in Nashville's Centennial Park waiting for my boys, Conner and Cayden, to come running into view just before they cross the finish line of their first triathlon.

I don't have any idea where they are in the park, but when I close my eyes I picture Conner, his cheeks red and his blond hair matted with sweat, smiling and waving to the hundreds of people who line the racecourse. I see Cayden too, with his eyes closed feeling the breeze across his cheeks as he sits in that low, blue running stroller, being pushed by Conner. I imagine him clapping as he does when he's really happy, and I know he's happy now as he glides along, cheered by everyone who sees him and his brother pass.

"Look," those parents are saying to their children, "look at what one brother can do for another. That's what family is all about."

Two weeks ago we had never even watched a triathlon, let alone thought about entering one. But when Conner heard about a sport where you biked, swam and ran all in one race, he wanted to do it, and he wanted to bring his brother Cayden along for the ride.

Conner is just 7 years old. He's never run or biked in a race. The only swimming stroke he knows is the dog paddle. Cayden is 5, still tiny and frail on account of his cerebral palsy.

To outsiders, Cayden can seem like he's lost in the universe, his hands drifting back and forth in front of his torso as if he's reaching for something he can't find. His head moves to its own rhythm, and he never seems to be looking at anyone or anything in particular. But when Conner talks, Cayden listens. He lifts his head and looks Conner right in the eyes. Even though Cayden cannot speak in words, I know he speaks to Conner.

Other brothers ride their bikes down to the creek, race across the tall summer grass to see who's the fastest, and stay up late trading secrets and jokes by the glow of flashlights. Cayden and Conner can't do any of that, yet Cayden is the reason Conner entered this triathlon in the first place. He wanted to find a way to do something with his brother, something just for them.

To do this together, though, Conner would have to carry Cayden every step of the way, pulling him in a raft as he swam, wheeling him in a trailer attached to his bike and, finally, pushing him in a stroller over the finish line. To me, it seemed impossible! More than four miles of swimming, biking and running, all back-to-back-to-back, through heat, exhaustion, hills and valleys. But Conner just locked in and kept on going. That's what he's doing right now somewhere on that racecourse: He and his brother are finding their way to the finish.

Kids of all ages and sizes are sprinting by me. A race announcer is calling them all home.

"Way to go!" he says in a booming voice. "Here she comes!"

These kids are awesome. Their parents are beaming, giving out hugs and high fives. All I see is joy. But *my* boys haven't finished yet.

Relax. Breathe. They're fine out there. They're going to be fine.

The park is beautiful. Clear sky. Warm and humid, the way Nashville gets in early June. I could make you a mile-long list of reasons why my family and I shouldn't even be here standing among these people with their fancy race gear and their high-tech bikes. Some of these kids have been training for this event for years, and mine started just last week. Me and my husband Jeff don't fit in with these fine, upstanding people. Can they tell we feel uncomfortable and out of place? There are television crews and newspaper photographers standing with me here at the finish, waiting to capture the moment when the boys cross. They tell me our story is an inspiration. I wonder how they'd feel if they knew the *whole* story.

More kids pass me by. More waiting. Didn't I see that little girl start the run after the boys? Where are they? Are they going to make it?

Wait. Now I think I see them. Yes, there they are, I see them breaking through the trees down 25th Avenue. That's Conner. His eyes just clear the push bar of the jogging stroller. He's grinning and whooping. Cayden is smiling, too, and clapping. I'm crying. I see Jeff now. He's back by my side, and his eyes are rimmed red. He's so proud.

Conner looks like he's getting stronger, pushing that stroller the last few steps.

"Look at this!" the announcer screams. "This is incredible!"

My boys are going to make it. They're going to cross that line. When the day started, the only cheering section they had was me, Jeff and a few friends from our congregation back home. Now hundreds of people are cheering for them. It's loud. The love is overpowering. Cayden looks so happy. Conner carried his brother through this race, but Cayden is the one who pushed his brother to reach the end.

All these people, rooting for our boys. Again, I wonder: Are they really cheering for my family? Do they know who we *really* are?

chapter one

HOME

Cayden was only a few months old when the doctors diagnosed him with spastic cerebral palsy. Diseases like CP can have a wide range of effects, some symptoms severe and others less noticeable. In Cayden's case, they told us that he'd always have trouble learning, that he'd never walk, never talk and never be able to take care of himself or live on his own. We didn't sit Conner down to explain what the condition meant, because at first we really didn't know anything about it ourselves.

We all ended up learning about Cayden's CP together, as a family. For Conner, Cayden was always just Cayden, his brother who did things differently. Conner never asked why his brother was the way he was. The whys didn't matter to him. He loved Cayden for the person he was, not the person he wasn't.

Growing up with a brother with special needs had many positive effects on Conner. He learned never to judge. He learned compassion. When his brother needed extra time to get ready to leave the house, Conner learned to wait. When Cayden couldn't speak for himself, Conner learned to understand his brother's body language and what he was feeling so he could help speak for him. And when Cayden was teased or taunted for being different— Conner learned to speak up.

The bond my boys shared was special right from the start. In a word, it was family. I loved that. I loved watching their relationship grow stronger and deeper as the years passed, especially since family had been such a tricky thing for me to find in my own life. I had that feeling for a while—before it was taken away.

———

WHEN I WAS a little girl I loved to hear family stories about the way our hometown, Old Hickory, Tennessee, was when my mom was my age. The house where she grew up had been the center of our life for generations. To hear the family describe it, Old Hickory was like Mayberry on the old *Andy Griffith Show*. On the Fourth of July all the families set up lawn chairs to watch the fireworks. The men had an annual contest to see who could make the best flavor of hand-churned ice cream. The atmosphere was so ideal that everyone called it Pleasantville. Sure, it was a company town; everybody worked for DuPont, and nobody made much money. But the way my family told it, those were its strengths.

My mother's grandfather bought the little yellow duplex at the end of a cul-de-sac when it was new, passing it down from father to daughter to daughter ever since. My Nanny and Pop raised their children there, and when my mom's third marriage ended, we moved in. My mom and me lived on one side of the duplex, and my grandparents lived on the other. Anytime I wanted to see

Nanny or Pop, I just opened their unlocked door and walked in.

They always shook their heads when they talked about how things had changed in Old Hickory—too many renters were taking over; where was the pride?—but I still saw it as Pleasantville.

I remember the comfort and security of waking up next to my mom in her white wrought-iron bed in an all-white bedroom. We slept under a pale pink floral bedspread with hints of purple and green. I like to remember it on Sundays late in the spring. I woke up to sunbeams on my face and the sound of Pop outside watering his garden. I knew that when we came home from church, Nanny's kitchen would smell like tomato sauce, rich with herbs from Pop's garden. We'd all have Sunday dinner together. And my most precious Sunday morning memory of all is of a moment before the day even started, when I nestled in that magical nook by my mother's back, where I fit perfectly.

In some ways I thought I had it better in Old Hickory than Mom had. When she was little, Pop was working and couldn't wait outside the school building every day to walk her home, as he did for me. While he waited, Pop would peel me an apple that he'd picked from one of the trees at the end of the cul-de-sac. As we walked back to the duplex, I munched and chattered about the day at school. My grandpa never said much. He just smiled. As soon as we rounded the corner, I looked to see if the front door on our side of the duplex was open. If it was, I could usually see the silhouette of my mom as she moved around the kitchen. I wanted to be just like her, and—just like her—I expected to spend my whole life in Old Hickory. But it didn't turn out that way.

My mother was sick—really sick—twice during my childhood, and when she died I was only 12, too young to have a say in where

JENNY LONG WITH BOB DER

I wanted to be. The court ruled that I had to live with my father, a man I felt I barely knew. The only thing I knew for sure was that no one in Old Hickory had a good thing to say about him. My mother's death hurled me from that cozy white bedroom into a big and scary world. I went from feeling safe in my mother's bed to dangling by a thread.

In some ways, like other children of single moms, I had been dangling my whole life. But I couldn't get my feet back under me for years after my mother died. I dropped out of high school, got pregnant and was well on my way to becoming a sad statistic, until my boys turned it all around. They gave my life value and purpose and showed me our little family was worth fighting for. And when they entered that race, when they crossed the finish line and the whole world started cheering, I finally knew that I didn't have to feel ashamed.

It's hard for me to remember a time when my mom wasn't sick. I was 5 years old when she was diagnosed with breast cancer and the adults started speaking about her in hushed voices, trying to protect me from the truth. I was shuttled around from staying with my Aunt Susan, my mom's younger sister, to my godmother Donna, my mom's best friend from high school. They tried their best to make the nights away from home seem like fun sleepovers, but pizza and coloring books couldn't hide the expressions on their faces.

All the adults were racing around, crying and sending me off from one house to another. That meant something was really wrong. I knew it.

Sometimes they would take me to visit my mom at Vanderbilt Hospital. They tried so hard to make it not scary for me. I still remember the little "playground" in the hospital lobby. It was just a plastic jungle gym set up on the carpet. But I was always steered over there so it would feel like I was out to have fun and not see my sick mother. I did as I was told. I went up and down that plastic slide. But this wasn't like any other playground I had ever visited. It was cold, and it smelled weird. I knew something was wrong. No one had to explain it to me. I felt it.

That's why I firmly believe that you can't hide troubles from a child, even a young one. Children know a lot more than their parents think they do, and are capable of understanding a lot more, too.

I spent the summer before kindergarten with a relative in California while my mom endured a brutal round of chemotherapy to fight the cancer. Of course I was anxious to get back home to see my mom and to start the adventure of big-kid school. But my mom wanted to be stronger before we saw each other, so I missed the first few weeks. When my grandparents finally brought me back from the airport, I raced up the stairs to see my mom. I ran to her and held her, at first very lightly. She was so thin, but she was still strong. I felt her strength in the way she hugged me back and because it seemed like her kisses would never stop. It was only when I looked up from the comfort of her arms that I noticed her hair—short, spiky and blond—was the complete opposite of her natural, lush chestnut curls. She was wearing a wig.

I wanted to ask my mom a million questions, but all she wanted to talk about was my adventure in California.

"How was the beach? Tell me about Disneyland!"

This was my first lesson in how little Mom wanted to dwell on her cancer. She knew how sick she had been—no need talking about it. She just wanted light and life and hope. Providing those things was my job. It was quite a heavy lift for a little girl. But she was my family, my home, my everything—so we didn't talk about sickness but instead focused on getting me ready for my first day of school.

Mom was coming with me to class and staying all day. That sounded perfect. I had spent so many nights worrying about her and how she was doing, worrying about when—or if—I would get to see her again. Now she was here, whole and happy and ready to take me to school in the morning. Maybe she'd be there every day, I thought. Maybe we could do everything together.

When I woke up the next day, she was already out of bed, all dolled up in finery she'd gotten at the Goodwill. Along with the wig, she had big clip-on hoop earrings, coral-red lipstick and eye shadow. It was like I was going to the first day of kindergarten with a movie star.

My mom had my lunch already packed, and we set out to walk slowly, steadily, the few blocks to school. I was so proud to enter the classroom holding her hand. She walked directly to the kindergarten classroom and introduced me to the teacher. Then the teacher introduced me to the class. When I took my seat, my mom sat by my side so I wouldn't be scared.

That fall, the two of us were closer than ever. Mom was on disability from work, so she was always home when I got back from school. Often we'd walk together to the Piggly Wiggly to shop for groceries, choosing carefully because we were on a budget: lots of Vienna sausages and boxes of mac and cheese. At night we propped up the pillows on the big white bed so we could watch *The Golden Girls* on the TV that sat on a bookshelf in the closet. Most nights I drifted to sleep to the sound of her laughter. Life seemed perfect. I thought there'd be nothing but clear skies, open doors and lazy Sundays up ahead.

— chapter two —

EXPECT
A MIRACLE

I've always loved Centennial Park because it was the first place I really felt Jeff and Conner and me were becoming a family. From almost the day Conner was born, the three of us did pretty much everything together. Jeff loved Conner the first time they met. There was an ease about the way Jeff slipped into our lives when Conner's daddy dropped out. He understood how to soothe Conner and keep him smiling.

Summer weekends when the weather was warm, we'd bring a picnic to the grassy fields of Centennial Park so Conner could play and Schuyler, our Siberian husky, could chase down a few butterflies.

That first summer, when Conner was just a baby, he and Jeff would roll around on the grass while I lay back soaking in the sun. The next summer, when Conner was closing in on 2, Jeff taught him how to play catch and how to get the ball back from Schuyler. By that time, me and Jeff had a child of our own on the way. I remember that afternoon as one of the happiest moments of my life, resting back on the blanket in the freshly mowed grass on an early summer evening as I waited for Conner and Jeff to join me. As soon as they got tired of playing catch, we were going to tell Conner that he was going to be a big brother.

I watched Conner and Jeff toss the ball while Schuyler ran back and forth between them, hoping desperately that someone would drop it. I lay on my back, looked at the sky and rubbed my belly. I thought about how my body was about to change as I brought another life into this world. And I thought about Conner. Conner was the one who'd brought me and Jeff together in the first place, and this little baby would cement us as a family.

IT TOOK SIX YEARS for my mom to get sick again, but when she did, her decline was sudden and dramatic.

I was almost 12 years old when it started to happen again. This time I sensed it before they told me. I still slept with my mom. Most mornings she woke up first and got me up with a kiss and a gentle nudge. But one day, not long before my birthday, I woke up out of a dream in a panic.

In my dream, I was staring at my mother while she lay sleeping. She looked beautiful. Her hair had grown back into curly brown ringlets that fell around her face. The sunlight picked up all the blond and red undertones. She looked serene and healthy. Then I looked back at her in my dream state and realized she wasn't sleeping in bed at all—she was lying in a coffin.

I woke up sharply. I reached over to place my hand gently on my mom's head, hoping that touch would bring me back to the reality of the room we shared. I hoped it would make my bad feelings go away.

"Please don't ever get sick again and leave me," I whispered, more like a prayer than anything else. I was talking to myself and to my mom, but I was pleading with God. "Please don't ever die."

My mother's eyes opened, and I was startled. She reached out her arm and pulled me close.

"I'm not going anywhere," she assured me as she stroked my hair and rocked me gently. "Mama's fine. No matter what happens I'll never leave you. I'll always be at your side."

I knew she meant it, and I wanted to believe it was true. But soon she was ill again, very ill. Within a few days her skin became chalky and pale. When she did simple things like clearing the table or folding the laundry, she had to stop and take a rest.

I kept offering to help her, but she wouldn't let me. I was very frightened of what was happening, and she kept trying to protect me. When I asked her how she was feeling, she never gave me a real answer.

Finally, one day, she simply announced that she needed to go to the hospital for some tests. We had made other plans—but sometimes life laughs at your plans. For weeks we were preparing a big 12th-birthday party for me, a grownup party at the house instead of a little-girl party at the skating rink like I usually would have. We had a menu picked out and invitations too, but I didn't want my mom to exhaust herself pulling together a party for me. She needed all of her strength for herself.

"Mommy, you don't have to throw me a birthday party," I blurted out as soon as she told me about the hospital. "It's too much right now. You're not strong enough."

"No," my mother said firmly, shaking her head. "I'll be fine. I promised you this party, and we're going to find a way."

If I could travel back in time, I'd go to that room and hug my mom so tight. I'd tell her how much I love her, tell her how her words that we could "find a way" have stayed with me my whole life, through all the ups and downs. I'd tell her that I try to teach my own children the same thing—we'll find a way—and how that belief has carried us further and higher than I could ever have imagined. But I don't have a time machine, I just have my memories, and what I remember is how weak and tired my mother looked, scared of dying, though still the strongest person I have ever known.

The day of my birthday party, I was so proud to live in Pleasantville. Our neighbors and friends rallied around my mother to help her throw my party. People stopped by with cookies and Rice Krispies Treats, paper plates and cups. Pop worked the grill, cooking hot dogs and hamburgers. Nanny helped my mom finish decorating the birthday cake.

As I blew out the candles, I wished for just one thing: for the tests at the hospital to go well and for my mom to come home healthy. On my actual birthday, the day my mom had her tests, it seemed like maybe my wish was going to come true. The doctors treated her and sent her home within a week. I remember walking back from school the day she was released and finding the front door wide open. I was so happy and relieved she was home. Nanny and Pop told me, "Your mom is all better!"

But Mom wasn't herself.

Another day, soon after, I came home to find that she had pulled up a chair next to the stove to stir a pot of canned soup for my afternoon snack because she didn't have enough strength to stand. I tried my best to be more helpful with chores. I figured anything I could do to ease the pressures on my mother and give her more chance to rest would help her stay healthy.

"Mom, I know how to do a lot of things," I told her. "I can do the shopping. I know how to get to the Piggly Wiggly. I know what we need. I know how to clean. I can help."

My mom wasn't having it. She didn't want me to have to carry out what she saw as her responsibilities as a mother.

"You don't have to do that, sweetheart," she would tell me. "I'm gonna be fine. I'm getting better every day."

I wanted to believe her, I wanted to so badly, but I was also scared that no matter how much I wanted her to be healthy and to stay with me, my wishes were no match for what was happening to her body. My mom had had plenty of tests over the years, and most of them showed how well she was doing after beating breast cancer. But now she was fighting leukemia, a disease that prevents the body from making enough good blood cells to fight disease and infection. The doctors said the leukemia was probably brought on by the aggressive chemotherapy they'd dosed my mom with to fight breast cancer six years before.

Every day I watched as the leukemia ravaged my mother's body. She would spend a few days in Vanderbilt Hospital for treatment, then come home for a few days in between. I slept next to her when she was home, but her body was so weak and frail, I thought I would snap her if I held her too tight. Her entire body was soon covered with bruises caused by her condition—but sometimes I worried that maybe they were caused by my hugging her too much. It hurt her to stand, to walk, even to move. All of her energy was gone. The safety I always felt lying next to her was slipping away, and the feeling that replaced it was dread.

When people are really sick like my mom was, they sometimes

have a moment of euphoria before they die. A strength overcomes them, and they start acting like an exaggerated version of the person they used to be, the person they were before they were sick. That happened to my mother once between stays at the hospital. She simply woke up one day, got out of bed like there wasn't a pain in her body and started looking around the living room.

"I'm sick of this," she told me, waving her arm at the tattered sofa and the wobbly chairs. "I think we need new furniture."

I was shocked. I didn't know what to say. It was like a miracle recovery.

"They always say at church that the Lord will provide," she said. "Well, I think it's time for the Lord to provide us with some new furniture. Jenny, get ready. We're going shopping."

My mother asked a friend from the neighborhood to drive us. Mom slipped on the paper mask the hospital gave her to protect her from germs, and grabbed my hand.

"Let's go!" she said. "We're going to Walmart, and you can have anything you want."

When we got to the store, she was joyful as she grabbed a wide cart and pushed it down the aisles. A new set of pots and pans? Sure. Towels. Linens. Scented candles. I was right beside her, fearful that she was going to fall over and that I would have to brace her body before it hit the ground.

We rounded the corner to the furniture department, and my mom tossed aside all restraint. We picked out a whole new living-room set—a sofa, a recliner, the works. At the checkout, my mom told the cashier to put it all on credit. That was all it took. The whole purchase went through without a hitch, and it didn't seem to matter that we didn't have the money for all the things we bought.

I felt as though we'd become other people, people with so much money that they could spend it on whatever they wanted. I'll never forget the joy of racing together down the big aisles. She was pushing that cart, and I could see the freedom on her face. My mom was always so careful with money. We made the most of every dime and savored the smallest treats, like Popsicles or two-for-one fast-food hamburgers. But for one giddy evening, we didn't think about what we couldn't do in life. We just lived.

The next day when I returned home from school, the front door to our side of the duplex was closed. Mom was getting ready to be admitted to Vanderbilt again, and by the quiet tension that filled the house, it didn't seem like she would be returning home soon.

As my mom was packing her things to leave for the hospital, she called me into the bedroom.

"I want to give you something," she said, patting the spot next to her on the bed so I would sit next to her. "It's a birthday present."

Mom pulled out a box wrapped in beautiful pink and silver paper with a silver ribbon tying it together. She moved so slowly that I think it took all of her strength to offer this little jewel of a present up to me. I could see on her face how proud she was, how much this gift meant to her, and my heart swelled. She was going to the hospital, but she was thinking about me.

I carefully untied the ribbon and gently broke the seal of the tape that held the paper in place. I pulled off the top of the box and separated the pink tissue paper. Inside was a glittering, gleaming snow globe.

I held it up next to a lamp and wondered at how beautiful it was. Up against the light, I saw individual flakes of snow twirling in the liquid. Each flake sparkled in the light like a tiny, twinkling wishing star.

"It's so pretty," I said, hugging the snow globe to my chest. "Thank you, Mom."

My mother carefully took the globe into her hands. Her fingers were so thin that it looked like she had no flesh at all on them, and bruises ran from her wrists all the way up her arms. She set the snow globe on the bed between us and twisted the glass bulb.

"See, it plays music, too," she said.

I watched the fairy godmother inside spin and saw the glitter flutter around her angel wings. Bending slightly at her waist, she waved a magic wand in a delicate storm of tiny white sparkles as she twirled. A tinkling, music-box version of "When You Wish upon a Star" played. My mom's thin finger traced across a message written in gold script around the base: EXPECT A MIRACLE.

Expect a miracle. I prayed every night for a miracle that would make my mom healthy again. In church we had been schooled in the power of faith and prayer. I wanted that miracle with all my heart. My mom needed to believe it, too. She had to somehow find the strength to fight this disease. She made a miraculous recovery before, and I believed she was going to do it again. I realize now it wasn't as simple as that. Maybe my mom knew that it was too late for a miracle to save her life—but still, she never wanted me to give up hope that when times got tough, somehow I was going to have a happy ending.

I felt a big, hard lump in my throat, but I held back my tears. Instead of breaking down, I decided to be strong. That's what my mom did every day trying to protect me from the pain of what was happening. I needed to protect her, too, from my sorrow and my feeling that I was about to lose her, the only home I'd ever had.

My mom would essentially live the next four months of her life within the walls of Vanderbilt Hospital. The bruises were all over her body, blistering until they burst and stained her sheets. She was bald again, and sometimes she would vomit up stuff that looked like pitch-black tar. She'd get diarrhea, too, and being too weak to use the bathroom, she'd use a portable toilet that they set up next to her bed. Sometimes I'd have to help her clean up.

While she was in the hospital, I was living out of a duffel bag, carrying only my clothes for school and my snow globe. Aunt Susan and Donna both took me in for stays, just like they had when I was 6. Every night when I went to sleep, I took out my snow globe and prayed for the miracle—the miracle to save my mother, to save my family.

We were always regular churchgoers on Sunday mornings, but after mom got sick with breast cancer and came home healthy, we started going to a different church, and going more often. Mom was grateful to God that she had made it through, and I think she wanted to feel the power of the Holy Spirit moving through her, making her strong and free from disease.

She believed that this church has saved her from cancer, all her sins had been forgiven and she was reconciled with God. She taught me that to follow the Bible was to practice every word. To be good Christians we had to follow its teachings to the letter and obey all the commandments. My godmother Donna was a member of this church too, and it was something we all did together.

With Sunday school, the adult services that followed and Wednesday services too, I started speaking in tongues sometimes myself. I believed what we heard in church, that Jesus could cure the sick with the laying on of hands. I'd seen it happen where people prayed and laid hands on the sick and healed the person right there. Mom believed that prayer had been just as powerful a force in her getting better from the cancer as the work the doctors did. I believed that, too. I believed everything had worked together to bring my mom back home to me. I don't think I've ever prayed any harder than in the four months when my mom was in and out of the hospital. Everyone in the church kept my mother in their prayers. With all those people praying, I believed God would hear us.

The doctor's last hope was to replace my mother's bone marrow with that of a healthy person so her body could start making good blood cells again, the kind that fight off infections. The doctors said it was tough to find the right donor because the donor's bone marrow had to match perfectly. When they discovered that Aunt Susan was a match, I thought that maybe my prayers had been answered.

But even with Aunt Susan's marrow in her, my mother's condition continued to worsen. More blisters. Worse trouble breathing after one of her lungs collapsed. Her body was shutting down on itself, and I could see the fighting spirit dimming in her eyes whenever I went to the hospital to visit.

I went often, or as often as I could get someone to drive me there. Sometimes they'd just drop me off, and I'd make my way through the big hospital corridors on my own. I knew the way. When it was just me and Mom, I climbed into her hospital bed to lie next to her. I would pretend that we were in our white iron bed back in Old Hickory, but there was no comfort in this room. It didn't smell like my mom's potpourri, all apples and cinnamon. It smelled like antiseptic cleaner, chemicals and medicine.

The week before my mom died, I came home from school and

heard Nanny on the phone with Walmart arranging to send all the furniture back. I knew it meant my mom wasn't coming home. I couldn't bear to go into our side of the duplex. I wanted to remember that joy of the crazy night we bought it all, and to hold in my heart a memory of my mom and me being free and happy. I needed to see my mom right away, but neither Nanny nor Pop wanted to take me to see her.

I called my half brother Tucker, who was 16 years older than me and already a man. I knew he would help me if he could. I asked him to drive me to see her and that he spend time with her, too. That would make her happy.

"Come out now, Jenny? She's resting."

"Please, Tucker. Please. I must see her. You need to come get me. I'm begging you, please."

Tucker picked me up, and as I got out of the car in front of the hospital I looked back and saw that Tucker wasn't coming with me.

"You have to come up there, Tucker. Don't you want to see Mom?"

"I'm going to park and wait for you in the car."

"You can't do that, Tucker. Please come up with me. She wants to see you, too."

Tucker drove off to the parking lot, and I went in alone.

When I entered her room on the 11th floor, Mom was asleep. I sat down in a chair and just watched her. I shut my eyes and prayed, imagining her all better with vibrant skin, just like she'd had a few months ago, and a full head of hair. When I opened my eyes, something moved me to stand up.

I walked to her bed, and I laid my hands on her thin, weak body. I called up to the power of God, and I felt Him moving through me to heal my mom, just as I had watched people do in church. I closed my eyes and called up to Jesus with all my might, trying so hard to bring that miracle to my mother's diseased body that I felt like I might faint.

"Please don't let my mom die. Please don't take her away from me. I need her. I need her."

Minutes passed before I opened my eyes to see Tucker standing in the doorway. He looked like a bear, big-bellied and bearded. The sight of my mom so sick and me praying over her was all too much for him, and he quickly turned to walk away.

"C'mon, Jenny," he said. "We gotta go."

Mom's last time at the duplex was when she came home briefly, right before Valentine's Day. She was too weak to talk much, but we both pretended that everything was like it always had been. I kept my sorrow and fear inside so I could concentrate on holding on to every moment with her.

We ate a simple dinner together, then stayed up late watching TV in the white iron bed, just like we used to do. I had been saving money to buy her a special gift. Aunt Susan drove me to Walmart so I could get her a gold necklace that said NO. 1 MOM. I didn't have quite enough money, but Aunt Susan helped me make up the difference.

That last night, I sat with Mom in bed while she opened the box. She touched the necklace gently with her index finger and looked at me with eyes filled with love. I took the necklace out of the box and helped her clasp the chain behind her neck.

"I love you," she said in a voice as small and thin as she had become.

"I love you, too."

My mother died on February 18, 1995. She was 45 years old.

When I woke up early the next morning and saw Donna sitting on the edge of the bed, I knew what had happened before Donna spoke.

"She passed," Donna said, gently stroking my head, her eyes downcast and tired, red from crying.

I felt lost. I got up, got dressed and silently followed Donna to her car.

The backseat was filled with my mother's clothes from Vanderbilt. Everything smelled like the hospital, that cold, awful, chemical smell. I wasn't sure where we were going, but it didn't feel like it mattered much anymore. There weren't going to be any miracles for me. I was 12 years old, and it felt like I no longer had a family or a home.

— chapter three —

TRY

Cayden was born on October 10, 2005. Soon after he was delivered, the doctors told us that he was having trouble breathing on his own and needed to be hooked up to a ventilator until his lungs were strong enough.

"It's not uncommon," they told us. "Nothing to worry about. He'll be fine."

Sure enough, a few days later we were able to drive Cayden home from the hospital. All seemed well. He had a clean bill of health and an angelic face that radiated peace as he slept.

When we walked through the front door with Cayden in his bassinet, Conner was eager to meet his baby brother—but also a little hesitant. This was the first time Conner actually got to meet Cayden after all those months of talking about him.

Conner approached the bassinet like a boy creeping up behind Santa Claus. He looked nervous and cautious. He stopped *about three feet from his brother and peeked inside the bassinet.*

"It's O.K.," I said to Conner, waving him to come closer.

Conner nodded, then slowly walked up and gave Cayden a kiss on the forehead. Conner was 3 years old. He really didn't have any experience around a baby.

Conner stared at Cayden as he slept. They shared the same sandy blond hair, but they looked different. Cayden looked like Jeff, with a longish face and ears that stuck out a little. Conner was growing up to look a lot like me.

"Mom," he finally asked, "is it O.K. if I pet him?"

I laughed out loud.

That night, Conner showed the only jealousy toward his brother that I've ever seen from him. While Jeff and I cooed over the new baby, Conner refused to take a bath or eat dinner. An immovable pout hung around his lips, and he demanded our full attention.

I went over to Conner and rubbed his back as I hugged him.

"It's not always easy being a big brother," I said. "Sometimes Cayden will get more of our time. Sometimes you'll get more."

"What if I don't want to share?" Conner asked.

"I need you to try, O.K.? Just try."

WHEN WE ARRIVED at Donna's house, I went straight from the car to my godmother's bed without stopping to look back. I felt weak and light-headed. Under the covers, all I could do was sob until there were no tears left in me. I buried my face in the bedspread, light-headed and dizzy. My eyes hurt. Everything ached.

I had questions but no answers. Why did God have to take away my mom? She was good. She went to church. She lived according to the Bible—she tried to, at least. Eventually I fell into a deep sleep that swallowed me whole. I never wanted to climb out of it. I didn't want to face the world.

In my heart, I wanted to be strong and brave like I remembered my mom being, but the rest of my body just wanted to give up. Donna finally woke me to get dressed for the viewing at the funeral home.

A long stream of people from Old Hickory hugged me and patted me on the head as we walked in. They all meant well, but there was also pity in their eyes. I know everyone had their hearts open to me, but I felt so low, and all those eyes only made me feel worse.

"Poor Jenny Lynn," they would say as they turned away from me, thinking I couldn't hear them. "What's going to happen to her?"

I didn't want to go into the funeral parlor. I was terrified to see my mother's body, and terrified of the memory of my dream of her in a coffin that was about to come true. But I knew what was expected of me, so I forced myself to walk up to the casket.

My mother looked just like she did when she was sleeping, her face surrounded by peaceful light. But there was no warmth, no spirit—yet I felt some part of her was reaching out to me. She wore the necklace that I had given her just days before, the necklace that said NO. 1 MOM.

My mother was always going to be No. 1 for me. She was my role model, the person I looked to for guidance in those moments when I was smart enough to recognize I needed help. In death, she became my guardian angel, the spirit I would try to conjure up whenever things were tough or I felt confused. After her death, I made my decisions based on what I thought my mom would do in the same situation. That instinct made me strong, but I recognize now that I also used her spirit to justify some of the risky things I wanted to do. As a grieving 12-year-old, I took comfort in the idea of my mom's spirit guiding me along in life. As a teenager, I created an idea of her in my head—her kindness and love mixed with a general permissiveness that I probably made up in my own mind—and I used that idea to rationalize a lot of bad behavior. The idea of "what would Mom do?" became my strength and my weakness.

After the burial, there was a small reception at the funeral home. I planted myself on a stool in the kitchen, trying to disappear behind plates of cold cuts and cookies. I craved sleep. I wanted to go back to sleep for a week if I could. I thought that maybe if I could sleep that long, some of this terrible feeling would be gone when I woke up. Then Aunt Susan came to tell me that my father had arrived.

I didn't really know my father, Craig Yount. I can't remember living in the same house with him or anything about the time he and my mom were married. My mother tried to keep my dad in my life after they divorced. We had weekend visits for a while, but I don't remember those a whole lot either. Eventually he moved to Florida to start a jet-ski business. I didn't see him very often after that, even though he tried to stay connected to me with phone calls and planned visits that I worked my hardest to avoid.

"Tell him I can't visit this holiday," I would plead to my mother. "Tell him I'm sick."

"Give him a chance," my mother would tell me. "Try."

My mother never said a bad word about my dad in front of me. She respected the fact that he was my father, and she wanted me to love him and build my own relationship with him. Everyone else in my mother's family didn't speak well of him—and to be fair I didn't know what was true and what wasn't. All I knew was that being around the man made me uncomfortable.

As I walked down the funeral-parlor hallway to meet him, the man I saw standing in his suit seemed like a stranger. I didn't know how I'd react if he reached out to hug me. I never felt relaxed around my father. He was always so tense and, with his big booming voice, a little frightening to me.

"Hi, Baby," he said. He walked toward me with his arms open to give me a hug.

I stiffened.

"Hi."

"I'm sorry about your mom. She was a good woman, and she loved you more than anything. She fought real hard, Jenny. Real hard."

"Yeah." I looked off into the distance.

"I know I've been away awhile, but I did it for everyone's good."

I didn't know how to respond to that. How could going away be good? My mom was gone, and she wasn't coming back. There was nothing good about that.

"But I love you, Jenny Lynn. You're my girl, and I'm going to move back here from Florida to take care of you."

I didn't know where I wanted to live, but the last thing I wanted, the absolute last thing I could possibly imagine happening, was to leave Old Hickory and move in with my dad.

For the next two weeks, I stayed with Donna and mourned my mom. During the days, I'd sometimes go over to see Nanny and Pop or Aunt Susan because they were just six blocks from Donna's house. I was missing so much school that the teacher told Donna I was falling behind. I didn't care.

Meanwhile, a war was raging around me, a war between my dad and Donna for my custody. They both wanted me, and they both hired lawyers to get me. They were going to take this matter to court, and I felt like a pack of hamburger meat, raw and falling apart, being thrown between two barking dogs.

As the date drew closer, I was terrified that the judge would force me to leave Old Hickory and live with my father. He had moved back to Tennessee full time and was living with his mother at her ranch in Mount Juliet. Donna told me that all I had to do was tell the judge where I wanted to be, and he would follow my wishes.

"It's that simple," she assured me.

It wasn't that simple.

The hearing at the Sumner County courthouse was held on a sunny spring day. I felt itchy and tied up tight by the formal blouse and skirt that Donna had me wear. In the courtroom my mom's family sat together on a bench. All dressed up, they looked like they had at the funeral a few weeks before. On the other side sat my father.

When our case was called, Donna's lawyer entered into evidence a sheet of paper signed by the shaky hand of my dying mother. That paper was Donna's only proof that it was my mom's wish for me to be with her. The argument my dad's lawyer made was much simpler: Craig Yount was alive and living in Tennessee, and he was my birth father.

When the arguments were done, the judge looked at me. He must have seen how upset I was. He instructed me and the lawyers to meet with him in his chambers. As we entered his office, the judge took off his dark robe and hung it up. Then he lowered his big body into his big chair and looked me straight in the eyes.

"Where do you want to be, Jenny?"

"I want to be home."

"Your father and grandmother want to make their place your home."

"Please don't make me leave Old Hickory. That's all that I've ever known. I don't know my father, and he doesn't really know me."

"I understand, but he wants to get to know you."

"But I don't want to get to know him."

The judge leaned forward.

"Here's what's going to happen. You're going to stay with your godmother for the rest of the school year and finish sixth grade. Then, when summer starts, you're going to move in with your dad and give it a try. You have to give your father a chance. All right?"

That "all right" came down like the drop of a gavel.

While all my friends eagerly counted down the last few weeks of school before summer vacation, I did the opposite. Each day that passed moved me closer to leaving home and moving in with my father. I begged everyone to get me out of the situation— Donna, Aunt Susan, Nanny and Pop—but they explained again and again that they were powerless to go against the ruling of the court. The day before my father was supposed to pick me up, Donna sat me down for a talk.

"Look at the bright side," Donna said. "When you turn 18, you're an adult. There ain't nothing your father can do to keep you then. If I were you, I'd get a calendar and mark off the days until I was 18. Then I'd pack my bags."

The day my dad came to pick me up, I didn't have any tears left to cry. I carefully placed my duffel bag with all my belongings by the door as I waited for my father to arrive.

"You don't have to just stand there, Jenny Lynn. He's not here yet."

Donna was crying.

"No. I'm ready. I'll wait here."

My father double-parked his champagne-colored Cadillac Coupe DeVille. He knocked on the door, and Donna answered but didn't say a word. My father grabbed my bag, turned toward the street and walked down the pathway as I struggled to keep up with him. He opened the door for me and put my bag on the backseat, and I climbed in.

As we drove away, my father looked back at me in the rearview mirror and smiled.

"It's going to be good, Jenny," he said. "You'll see."

I looked back out of the rear window and saw my godmother standing in front of her house crying, waving goodbye. I stared out that window a good long while before I turned around to face reality.

— chapter four —

LOST

Conner always enjoyed being outdoors—fishing, riding his bike, playing in the park. He liked physical activity much more than any toy he could find in a store.

We encouraged Conner to be active. Living out in the country for most of his life allowed us to let Conner explore nature with his friends almost every day. It was easy to open the door and let him play in the yard while Cayden was napping.

Sometimes when the weather was nice, we'd go on little hikes. Conner enjoyed exploring and discovering new things. On one of our adventures, we walked so far and deep into the woods that I couldn't figure out the way back home. As I turned around and around, I started to worry. One tree looked the same as the next. Was the pathway up or down? I couldn't tell anymore.

"I think we may be lost," I finally said out loud.

I know there was panic in my voice. But Conner stayed calm. He wasn't looking to me for answers.

"We're not lost," Conner chirped. "I remember which way the creek was pointing. We just have to follow the creek and we'll get home."

That would happen more than once in our lives: I would make some kind of mistake and get us lost, and Conner would find the path to lead us back.

———————

As MY FATHER and I drove the 20 minutes from Old Hickory to Mount Juliet, both suburbs to the east of Nashville, I didn't say much. I looked at my father in the front seat of the Cadillac and shut my eyes trying to imagine what this new life would be like, but my imagination failed me. All I could think about was how it would never be as good, or even half as good, as the first 12 years with my mom.

When we pulled up in front of the ranch house, my dad couldn't wait to show me my new bedroom. He carried my duffel bag into the house and up a short flight of stairs to a tall room with an arched ceiling. Sunlight streamed through the windows, falling on a brand-new queen-size bed. The brass bed frame looked especially shiny against the light blue wall-to-wall carpet. That bed was just for me, and my dad had positioned a TV on the dresser close by. Next to the closet was a full-length mirror on a wooden stand so I could check my look before I left for school in the morning.

"It's nice," I said in a small voice, the first words I'd spoken since my father had picked me up in Old Hickory.

"Nice? It's great!" he said, and I saw the flash of a wounded look in his eyes. "Everything's brand new."

That was the problem: everything was new. I didn't even sit on the bed. I followed him downstairs to the living room, where we stood looking at each other in silence.

I spent the first night at my dad's house on the couch because I didn't want to wake up in that bedroom. In fact, I spent my first year sleeping on the couch. As nice as that bedroom was, I believed I could go my whole life without sleeping in there. The room had a new bed, a television and sunlight across the pillows, but it wasn't the bed I'd shared with my mom. I wasn't ready to accept anything less than that—anything less than the impossible.

Now that Conner is almost the same age I was then, I understand what being 12 means and how powerful that year is in the messy process of becoming an adult. I was still a little girl, and in many ways I acted a lot younger than 12. The death of my mom set me back years.

But in other ways, I was a lot older than 12, too. I had seen the ugliness of serious illness and experienced the loss of death. I toggled between the two sides of my personality—the needy, sad little girl and the world-weary young lady. I felt a sense of independence now that I had been cut free of everything I loved and valued, but at the same time I never stopped needing my mom to help guide my way. Since she wasn't there, I started making choices on my own and stuck by them in the same way I now see Conner make choices: determined, capable and persistent. I'd taken to heart my mom's "we'll make it work" attitude, and that part of me looked at life with my father simply as a practical arrangement. It was just a thing to get through. I didn't see any way I'd actually learn something from my father or benefit from being around him.

It's tough for even the best of parents to know how to guide a 12-year-old, let alone a little girl who has just lost her mom. My father wasn't ready for that—he had his own problems to deal with—and I sure didn't cut him any slack.

I tried to understand my father, but I failed at that more often than I succeeded. His intentions were usually driven by love, but he just wasn't an easy man for me to live with. He could be caring and gentle one minute, and harsh and overbearing the next. In a word, my father was complicated.

Growing up he was wild, which frequently landed him on the wrong side of his own father, a strict man who didn't tolerate nonsense. Nothing my father did seemed good enough for his dad, so after a while my dad stopped trying to please him and just had fun.

He was closer to his mother, a tough woman with a good mind for business. When he turned 16, my dad left home—mostly to get away from the fights between his parents. He enlisted in the Navy, but his service didn't last long. After the Navy he held a variety of jobs: salesman, radio DJ, small-business owner. The work was usually steady and played to his greatest strength: his ability to charm. Tall and muscular, with wavy brown hair that fell to his shoulders and a big brush mustache like Tom Selleck's, my father was a handsome man in a late-'70s kind of way. That was the man who charmed my mother, a woman who had a wild side of her own, according to my dad.

That first summer at my dad's house, the days quickly fell into a lazy pattern. I could sleep as late as I wanted or as long as I could hold out on that couch after my dad started moving around the house. Many mornings I pretended to sleep while I listened carefully to what he was doing. Eventually I'd get up, and after breakfast I'd lie out by the aboveground pool that my father had installed in the yard. When I got tired of the sun, Grandma would pile me in the car to go shopping.

No one seemed worried about money. Instead of thrift stores and tag sales, we shopped at the best stores in the big malls, name-brand stores like Express and Dillard's. Grandma would sit in a chair by the dressing room, urging me to take my pick of anything in the store.

The same with food. The first time I went to the grocery store with my dad, he told me to get anything I wanted. I picked the stuff I was used to eating: boxes of mac and cheese, jars of Vienna sausages or my mom's favorite brand of yogurt. When I tried to place my comfort foods in the cart, my father scowled.

"Why do you want that stuff? There's better stuff than that!" he said.

All this change was hard for me to take in. Vienna sausages, well, those were prized in the kitchen of Old Hickory, and somehow in Mount Juliet they were trash.

Another thing I quickly learned about living with my dad was that he liked to keep things tidy. My father put a lot of energy into maintaining a certain standard of cleanliness. He had a loud voice and wasn't shy about expressing his opinion, and he had opinions about things I didn't even know you could have opinions about. When I tried to make myself useful by doing some vacuuming and dusting, my father just about lost his mind.

"That's not how you vacuum, Jenny Lynn! You're missing spots everywhere. And you have to keep going over those areas two or three times if you really want to suck up all the dirt."

He came over and took the vacuum from my hands.

"You can't just go through the motions," he said without ever looking directly at me. "If you're going to do something, you have to do it right. Otherwise, don't even bother."

I didn't know what to say. I stood there frozen.

"Just go do something else," he said, brushing me aside as he started vacuuming over all the spots I had already done.

I decided that I would take my godmother's advice to heart. I made up my mind to be strong, to give my father a chance just like my mother and the judge had told me I should. If things were bad with my dad, on my 18th birthday I would simply walk out the door and start a life of my own.

After the summer was over and I was back in school, my dad started working again. He registered with the stagehand union so he could work the big concerts in Nashville—everyone from Johnny Cash to Alanis Morissette. Grandma lived in a smaller house nearby on the property and could look in on me, so my father and she decided I was old enough to take care of myself from time to time when he was working. I was a little scared at first, but I was also too scared to tell anyone.

When I came home from school, I never knew if he would be there or not. He might have gotten a call to work a show while I was in class. I also started to notice that my father liked to drink. If I saw a glass of cranberry juice in the kitchen, I knew there was vodka in there, too.

As the school bus turned the corner home, I'd look up to see whether his Coupe DeVille was in the driveway and try to prepare myself for what I was going to face when I turned the knob of the front door. This was nothing like the warmth of seeing my mom fixing a snack in the kitchen. My dad could be in any kind of mood. I stopped inviting friends home the night he pulled up as the pizza delivery guy was leaving. He was furious and accused us of trying to sneak a boy into the house.

The sad truth was, there were times I felt I couldn't do anything right around my dad. One night he came charging into the living room swinging a damp bath mat.

"You see this mat?" he asked. "Why is it so wet?"

"Because I took a shower?" I said.

"You dry off before you get out of the shower, Jenny Lynn. Any fool knows that."

My grandmother was a help, offering me a more predictable person to go to when things were rough with Dad. She would also scold him whenever his behavior got too close to the line. But even though she lived just steps away in the ranch's guesthouse, there was no getting around the fact that I was stuck with my dad—for better or worse. As the years passed, I started taking the approach my dad had with his own father—I stopped trying to do right.

When I was 15, I finally moved into the bedroom that my father had taken such care to set up for me. I wish I could say my reasons were pure, but the main reason I moved up there was that I could use the phone to make plans with my friends without his hearing. That spring at a party, I smoked my first Marlboro Light, and I was proud of myself because I barely coughed at all. It wasn't very long before I'd moved on to wine coolers and hard lemonade. Suddenly boys seemed very interested in me, and I was interested in them, too, especially the older ones.

That was the year I lost my virginity to a boy from school who I thought I loved. I didn't tell my father, but when that boy sent me roses at the house, my dad hit the roof. I just lied to him about having sex. I had sinned, but the world didn't open up beneath my feet and swallow me whole. So I sinned some more.

Where had my guardian angel gone? It pained me to realize that I wasn't thinking about my mom as much as I used to. I still missed her with all my heart, but she wasn't in my mind every minute of every day anymore. I guess my teenage mind was just too busy—a place of pure chaos. There were hormones surging through my body, the attention of the boys, the politics of the girls, schoolwork and all the little lapses and secrets that I needed to hide from my father—all those things took a lot of mental energy. I still had my snow globe in a prominent place on my dresser, but I rarely wound it up to hear my mother guide me to "wish upon a star."

The next line of that song is "makes no difference who you are." It did make a difference to me where I was. In Mount Juliet, I felt like I was on my own.

All those hours at church with my mom had taught me right from wrong. The Scripture had been drummed into my head in those twice-a-week worship sessions at Faith Is the Victory. But I strayed anyway. I was slipping in a glass or two of wine from the box my dad kept in the fridge. I was sneaking around behind my father's back to make out with boys.

Sin or fun? Suddenly the world didn't seem so black and white. Of course, somebody needed to talk sense to me. But even if they did, I was in no mood to listen. I was going to have to figure things out on my own, the hard way. That's not an excuse. It's a fact.

I did learn a lot by having so much freedom. I learned that's no way to raise a child. My boys will never get that kind of space with me, I promise you, because I know better than most how important it is for someone to be paying attention, to have someone who will keep a young person from following all the bad impulses that can so easily derail you.

When I turned 16, my godparents brought me along on vacation to Cancún. Lying on the beach the first day in my bikini, I was a 5-foot-7, blond-haired, blue-eyed woman who smoked, drank and had sex. In my mind, I was already a woman.

"Jenny Lynn, it won't be long before you can leave that house in Mount Juliet," Donna said. "I want you to know that if you do decide to leave your father, you'll always have a home with me."

I smiled and took a drag on my cigarette, counting the days in my head. I didn't realize that I was wandering deeper and deeper into the darkness.

— chapter five —

JUDGMENT

Jeff had given Conner a toy fishing pole as soon as he could stand. He showed him how to cast the line and reel in his catch. When Conner got a little bigger, he and Jeff would set off for the fishing hole on Saturdays, talking about what big fish they were going to catch. Jeff always found a way for Conner to catch something, which he presented so proudly to me. That is a precious memory to me, Conner looking up at Jeff as they hustled off to the car, his little legs doing double time to keep up, and both of them in their camo pants.

I worried that Conner would miss that special one-on-one time with Jeff once Cayden arrived, but it never bothered Conner. "When we go fishing, I'll teach my baby brother!" Conner used to say, waiting for the day when it could finally happen.

As the years passed, it became clear that Cayden would never be able to fully participate in that ritual with his father and brother. But Conner never lost his desire to find an activity they could share together. He never blamed Cayden or his CP for what they were missing out on. He just kept looking for a way.

———————

BY THE TIME I was a senior in high school, I'd made the transition from wounded 12-year-old to full-on bad girl. My grades were O.K., I was getting by, but I really wasn't putting much effort into my studies. My main concerns were going to parties in Nashville and spending time with my boyfriend, Travis.

Travis was several years older than me and played drums in an alternative-rock band. He liked to drink beers with his band buddies and just hang out, and I liked to do that, too. On weekends we'd crash at his house. Sometimes his mom would walk into his room and see the two of us passed out on his bed. I didn't dream of marrying Travis or anything, but it was easy and fun and got me out of the house—perfect for the 17-year-old me.

When I'd go home to Mount Juliet, I'd just walk in and go straight to my room to sleep. If my dad did anything to make me mad, I would cheer myself by thinking about my upcoming 18th birthday, the day I'd be able to finally leave my father's house for good and start my real life.

Sometimes, even on school days, I would stay out all night, and the day would begin with me asleep in the passenger seat of a friend's car with my knockoff Dolce & Gabbana sunglasses shading my eyes and my head resting against the cool glass. My eyes would be puffy and red as I greeted the dawn, still buzzing from too many Smirnoffs.

"Jenny. Get up. You're home."

I knew I looked like hell, but I didn't fear my father's

disapproval. I had the bad attitude of a rebellious teenager, and I was already making plans with my godmother to move out. She had a room in her basement for me that had its own bathroom and a separate entrance. Donna told me I could come and go as I pleased. It sounded ideal.

I had dreams for my future—immature dreams, but dreams. I imagined I would go to college, but I hadn't applied to any and my grades were a problem. If anyone asked me, my top choices were Tennessee and the University of Florida. I had heard that they had some good parties.

Another one of my goals was to have stuff. Things. High-quality things. After college, I wanted to get a job and earn real money. I'd watched how my Aunt Susan and her business partner bought run-down houses, fixed them up and then flipped them for a profit. It was an all-woman team, and I thought that was so cool. They were giving orders to contractors and getting things done. I saw checks on Aunt Susan's desk for $25,000 here and $30,000 there. I wanted a life like that. I wanted to live in a big loft in a city—any city. I wanted to go out with my friends and have romances and adventures. I felt like I had lived through enough sorrow, and now I just wanted to have fun.

My dad must have known that I was planning to leave because he tried to influence me to stay. First he told me he was throwing a big birthday party for me and all my friends at a hotel in downtown Nashville. Then he surprised me with a new car waiting for me in the driveway when I came home from school.

I didn't know what to say. I had been driving my father's old champagne Coupe DeVille ever since I was 16. It was fine for me, and I didn't want to owe my father anything, especially since I was planning to leave.

"You don't have to do this," I said.

"No, I want to get you that car. And the party, too. Now start getting ready to invite all your friends. I've reserved a suite at the Renaissance in Nashville. There's going to be food and everything."

Paying for a car and a party in the city was a huge gesture for my father, but it also annoyed me. He tried to win me over like that so many times. He could make me feel small and worthless day after day by nitpicking the way I did everything, then he'd wipe the slate clean with a gift in a box.

On the night of my 18th-birthday party, my father set up everything that I could have asked for in our suite at the hotel. There was plenty of food and soft drinks. Me and my friends sneaked in the beer and booze. Bouncing to the beat of Snoop Dogg and drinking our Smirnoffs, we thought we were a bunch of bad-asses. The liquor flowed, and our chaperone, my godmother, must have been fooled or looking the other way because she didn't lower any boom on us. Me and my friends all had big plans for life. Most girls talked about college. Others talked about meeting a great guy. I talked about leaving my father's house.

"Sure, you're going to leave," my friends said, rolling their eyes. They had heard me talk about this hundreds of times over the years.

"Oh, I'm leaving." I said. "You watch. I'm leaving tomorrow."

And that's exactly what I did. I drove back to the ranch the next day to drop off the keys to the new Kia Sephia my father had given me. My godmother followed in a U-Haul to help pick up my things.

My father didn't fight me or cause a scene. He just looked hurt as I went to my room to gather my belongings. I'd already packed everything before the party. As we drove away, the road stretched out in front of me and the path seemed to go on forever. I didn't even bother to look back.

It was incredibly cruel to leave my father the way I did. I can't bear to think of how much hurt I'd feel if Conner ever did that to me. But that decision didn't come without consequences. I paid for my foolishness. The decision to leave my father's home was the first domino to fall in a chain of horrible choices. By the time I realized I needed help, I was buried in a pit so deep it would take me years to claw out.

chapter six

I BELIEVED

I've always told the straight truth to my boys. I never sugarcoat my past. If I screw something up, I own up to it. If one of the boys does something wrong, like making a mistake in school or breaking a rule at home, we talk about it.

"Mom's not perfect," I often tell Conner. "I make mistakes. I've made lots of mistakes, even bad ones."

"I won't make any bad mistakes," Conner would sometimes say, his voice filled with confidence.

I knew that wasn't going to happen. I didn't even know if it would be normal to have a child who never made any mistakes. How would he learn and grow or reach his full potential if he never stretched for something and skinned his knees trying to reach it?

"Everyone makes mistakes," I tried to explain. "That's human, and it's O.K. to be human. You can always turn your mistakes around. You just have to learn from them and try to be better the next time."

AT FIRST, the basement bedroom at my godmother's house felt like a teenager's idea of heaven. At night I'd hang out with my boyfriend, Travis, shooting pool and drinking cheap beer. When I tired of Travis, I moved on to dating my godmother's nephew. She LOVED that. He was allowed to stay over because I think Donna believed we might get married and then I'd officially be part of her family.

True to her word, my godmother allowed me to come and go as I pleased. If I wasn't too tired or hung over, I'd go to school. If I didn't feel like going, I stayed home. Even when I was in school, I wasn't much good. I frequently dozed off in class.

I started getting comfortable following any impulse that flashed through my mind. I decided to break up with Donna's nephew and start dating Travis again for a while. Donna was hurt and mad that I'd dumped her nephew. Suddenly she tried to pull on my reins and impose a curfew on me. I didn't understand it, and I certainly didn't like it. If her problem was with my spending time with other boys, I just stopped doing it in front of her. Instead, I spent more time with my girlfriend Ashley, sleeping over at her house many nights so I could avoid the awkwardness with Donna.

I was in the homestretch of my senior year, but my grades were falling off terribly. I was flat-out failing math, and I would have to commit to summer school if I wanted to earn my diploma. If I had been motivated by my education, I would have just swallowed my pride and gone to summer school. But I was motivated by going to parties, and I was doing plenty of that already. So who needed college? I started imagining other ways that I could fulfill my dream of earning money. I thought maybe I could enroll in beauty school and become a hairdresser. Not just any hairdresser, though, but a famous one. Seriously. That was my new plan.

Oh my God, I was a mess.

One afternoon, just weeks before the end of the school year, Ashley and I were hanging out at the community pool wearing our shades and string bikinis. Sitting around, smoking Marlboros, we decided to go get tattoos. Soon I had the Chinese character for beauty inked on my pelvis. Then I made another decision.

"I don't want to go to school anymore," I proclaimed.

Ashley laughed. "Yeah. Let's drop out!"

I wasn't laughing. I was serious.

"I think I am going to drop out," I said.

"Don't be stupid, Jenny. There's two weeks left in school, and then we're done. Why would you drop out?"

"Because I want to go to beauty school."

Ashley laughed even harder. She wasn't the only one of my friends who thought I was being foolish. I just picked a day to quit and sneaked into the building late to turn in my books. A friend saw me and begged me to change my mind. "Don't drop out," she said. "We're so close to graduating." I didn't listen to her. I wasn't listening to anybody. I was focused and determined. I wanted to finally call all the shots for myself. It didn't feel like I had much support from anyone anyway—at least not support that mattered to me—so why not see how life would turn out when I followed my own instincts all the way?

That summer, I basically started living with Ashley at her parents' house. All my stuff was still at Donna's, but I was rarely there. I enrolled at a nearby beauty school—the Madison University of Beauty—and I started on all the basics: cutting, dyeing, set and curl. At night, I worked pouring drinks at a restaurant called Safari's. My salary helped pay for beauty school.

Things were working out well enough for me to feel like I had my life under control. But really I was just hanging on, vulnerable to being completely blown over if a strong enough force pushed against me.

Sure enough, that force arrived like a tornado in the form of BJ Green.

BJ was Ashley's older cousin. She had talked about him before in passing, how he was a troubled guy with a good heart. I'd never had the chance to judge for myself because he was in jail.

I was hanging out with Ashley, doing our usual, on the summer day when he was released. When he walked through the door, the first thing I noticed was his muscled arms. He wore a sleeveless T-shirt that showed them off, and he smelled good, a mix of olives and tobacco from his Armani cologne blended with his natural musk. The second thing I noticed about BJ was he had a sly, country-boy smile that sort of hung crooked on his face. He wasn't too tall, probably 5 foot 9, kind of stocky, with dark brown hair that he kept neat and tidy in a close crew cut.

"Who's this?" he asked his cousin.

"This is my friend, Jenny Yount."

"Nice to meet you, Jenny Yount. I'm Billy Joe Green, but you can call me BJ because that's what everyone calls me. Except my mom. She calls me an asshole."

I laughed. He was sexy and funny.

The rest of the day, BJ and Ashley and I just sat around wasting time and talking. At 23 years old, BJ not only had a police record, he had also developed a tolerance for jail time. He had confidence that he could survive any place and anything. Going to jail was no big deal to him. But he told his family that he didn't want to go back. This time, he said, he wanted to get something better out of life.

"I'm done with all that foolishness," he told Ashley's mom, his aunt and a woman I called Poppy. "I'm going to get a good job and make something of myself. I mean it, I promise you that."

I believed him when he said he wanted to change his life. I wanted my life to change, too, so who was I to judge BJ Green? Even in Old Hickory, I had grown up around people who had criminal records and had made mistakes in their past. They were still good people—churchgoing people who were able to turn themselves around to lead productive lives.

BJ told us he was going to get a job in construction; he already had a lead on work from a friend. I told BJ about beauty school.

"I'm sure you're really good at that beauty work," BJ said. "You've got style, anyone can see that. You're going to be famous one day."

"Yeah. O.K. Right."

"No, I mean it. You're special. I can tell that already, and I didn't even go to college."

By the afternoon, I told Ashley and BJ that I had better leave and get back to my godmother's place.

"Don't want to set off the alarm bells with Donna," I said, rolling my eyes as I got up from my chair. BJ stood up, too.

"I hope to see you around," BJ said with a smile. "It was really nice to meet you."

He looked me in the eyes as he said goodbye. I had seen that look before. It was the look a guy gives you when he's interested, a look that would make you feel uncomfortable if you weren't interested too.

That was the beginning of my crush on BJ, the kind of dangerous bad boy that parents warn their daughters to stay away from. The idea of being with a strong man who had a bit of the devil in him intrigued me. He was certainly a lot more interesting than the boys I had been dating. During the week while I was doing hair or tending bar, I thought of BJ and little else.

The next time I saw him, we found a quiet corner of Poppy's house where we could be alone and talk heart to heart. He told me how he would watch his parents fighting when he was a child and how sometimes his father would just disappear for a while. BJ's earliest memory was being 5 years old, sitting on the front stoop waiting for his father to come home. He waited a long time, long after dark, until his mother finally made him come inside.

BJ also told me that his mom was always on his case, constantly yelling at him for misbehaving and giving her trouble. He was already a rebellious kid, and her punishments made him wilder and more violent. He was in and out of lockup throughout his teen years, but that just made him even tougher. He started taking drugs and stealing money from his family to pay for them.

Since he opened up to me, I opened up to him. To most people, I'd come to tell the story of my mom dying in just a sentence, the simple fact that she had passed when I was 12. But it was different when I told BJ. He had a way of making me feel like I was the only other person he could depend on. I saw him as worldly, someone who could really understand the pain of my loss. I told him in detail about Old Hickory and my mom's cancer, and when I talked about her death I fell apart in tears in a way I hadn't allowed myself to do in years. BJ held me as I sobbed and I let out all that pent-up pain. In his arms, I felt safe.

When we parted that afternoon, I thought about how similar

we were. I could relate to BJ's childhood. He missed his dad just like I missed my mom. I started thinking that I could be the missing piece to make BJ whole again. And I felt that BJ could be the piece to make me whole again, too.

After only a month of knowing him, I considered BJ a close friend. When Ashley unexpectedly told me one morning that BJ was back in lockup after being caught drinking a beer at a bar—a direct violation of his parole—I asked if I could come with her to visit BJ in jail.

"BJ would love that," she told me. "You'll make his day."

I smiled. The idea that I could make BJ's day pleased me.

On the day of the visit, I went straight from beauty school, so I was wearing my scrubs, a cheap version of what they wear in hospitals. I went with Ashley, her mom and BJ's mother—all close members of his family—but the person he wanted to talk to most was me.

"What's Jenny doing back there? I can't believe you came here to see me," he said. "That really makes me happy. You have no idea. You look so beautiful. You look like a nurse."

BJ was laying the mack down on me from behind the bullet-proof glass! I started to blush. As we left the jail, I felt like a schoolgirl who had just spent time in the hallway talking to her crush. I couldn't wait for BJ to be released so I could be with him. For the first time in a long while, I didn't feel so alone in the world. I liked that feeling. I needed it.

chapter seven

15%

When Conner was about 6 years old, the sports bug bit him hard. He always enjoyed watching football with Jeff—sharing a love for the San Francisco 49ers—and one day he announced that he wanted to play a team sport, too. When we saw a flyer about sign-ups for a peewee basketball program at the rec center, we decided to let Conner give it a try.

Conner was so excited for the first day of practice. He had his team shirt on and was ready to go about an hour before we had to be at the gym. I had never seen that side of him before, the look of purpose and determination that was set in his eyes because he was really serious about something. That first day all of us went to practice—me and Jeff, Conner and Cayden.

We kept bringing Cayden with us to the gym for two or three basketball practices. Conner would always stand by his brother when there was a break, his hair tousled and his cheeks flush from all the running around. Conner explained to Cayden what the coaches *were teaching him on the court, how to set picks and shoot layups.*

Cayden would listen some, but he would get distracted, too, by the squeaks of all the sneakers on the shiny wooden floors or the bright, harsh lights that blazed overhead. When the breaks were over, Conner would go back to the team and Cayden would stay off to the side, away from the action. As I watched Cayden in his chair while Conner ran up and down the court, he never looked included. He looked lonely. Eventually he'd get so antsy that Jeff and I decided to have just one of us go to practice with Conner while the other stayed home with Cayden.

IN A RELATIONSHIP, what percent of the time spent with the other person is good? Most people don't count it up. You lose track when the relationship is long, and you don't even bother if the relationship is short. But I can tell you exactly what percent of my time with BJ Green was good: 15%.

That was the time we spent physically together, face to face, hand in hand, eye to eye. It includes the times we spent sitting on a couch watching TV, the times we hung out with friends having fun and the times we talked about the future. I had never met another person I believed in more passionately and completely than Billy Joe Green. I would do anything for him, go against anything I had been taught, because nothing since my childhood had ever delivered as much hope and fulfillment as those good moments spent with him: a precious, magical 15%.

For most people, 15% wouldn't feel like nearly enough happiness. But it was enough for me. I had grown so close to BJ so quickly because he needed me and he accepted me—and I needed him. When you added in the physical intensity of first love, I was willing to overlook just about anything.

While BJ was in jail he sent me dozens of letters, some of them with drawings: a portrait based on my school picture, my name in fancy script letters. The art was all in pencil on lined loose-leaf paper, like notes a boy would make in school. I thought the letters were romantic. Soon, BJ was paroled again. When I walked through the door at Ashley's house and he was waiting there with a grin on his face, I leaped into his arms. He was the one who had just gotten out of jail, but I was the one who felt free.

That night, BJ, Ashley and I celebrated by driving to the community pool with me and Ashley on the hood of the car. The lights at the pool were on, but the gate was locked. We scaled the fence and lay around drinking malt liquor and smoking cigars. We were all drunk, and if the police had been around, BJ would have gone straight back to jail. Guaranteed. But BJ didn't care. He liked the idea that he might just get away with all of his nonsense again. And that time, he did.

Soon we were all wading in the pool. After a few minutes of splashing around, Ashley stretched out on a deck chair to smoke another cigar. BJ and I stayed in the pool. His strong hands, thickened by the years he'd spent working construction, held on to my waist, and he brushed his mustache against the tender skin on my neck and shoulder as he moved around me in the water. Every time he brushed against me I shivered. He started teasing me about my tattoo—a little bit of it was visible around my bikini bottom.

"Do you have a tattoo, Jenny Lynn? I thought you were a good girl!"

I laughed.

"Yeah, I got a little tattoo. That don't make me bad."

"Yeah? Well, can I see it?"

"You see it, BJ. If you didn't see it, why'd you ask?"

"I mean up close. Here, I'll show you my tattoos."

BJ let go of my waist and walked a few feet away from me in the pool. He had a beautiful torso with ripped muscles and huge strong arms. I'd been smitten with the way he looked, but I'd never seen this much of him before. He turned around and showed me the word OUTLAW inked across his broad, strong back. It was impressive. Then he made his way to me, slowly, to get closer.

"Don't be afraid. I got to get real close for you to see this one."

BJ was practically nose to nose with me now. He wasn't saying a word, just looking deeply at me as he raised his hand and pointed to the corner of his eye. At the end of his fingertip I could see that he was pointing to a small tattoo in the shape of a teardrop.

"This one means I've seen hard times," he whispered.

"I have, too," I said.

"I know you have."

The water rippled softly around us, and the tiny hairs on my arms and neck were standing on end. I could feel the breeze and hear him breathing. I wasn't staring into his eyes anymore, I was melting into them. It felt like dying and flying and rising above my body, all at the same time.

I closed my eyes, and BJ broke the thin space of air between us to kiss me for the first time.

"Do you want to get out of here with me?" he whispered in my ear.

"Yes."

We left the pool with Ashley and went back to Poppy's house. Ashley passed out on the sofa in the basement while BJ and I sneaked off to the guest room to make love for the first time. We fell asleep holding each other.

———

No ONE ELSE I knew liked what they saw in BJ Green. My godmother, Donna, absolutely hated him. My friends warned me about him, too. They whispered all the small-town gossip into my ear, how he had been married and had a daughter, how that other woman had to leave him because he was so wild and violent.

Other people's doubts drove me to BJ with even greater conviction. They didn't see him the way I did. They didn't understand him. They weren't around for the 15%. BJ was going to prove everyone wrong, I knew it, and I was going to be the one to help him because I loved him.

When BJ suddenly asked me to move in with him one night, surrounded by his friends sitting in a booth at Chili's, I was shocked. And thrilled.

"I think that sounds really, really good," I said.

BJ was so happy—and so wired. We hugged like he had just asked me to marry him. The next day we started looking at apartments. Everything was happening so fast—too fast—but I didn't know how to slow it down. Maybe I didn't want to.

We looked at a lot of nasty apartments that day: garden apartments, shabby two-family duplexes, places by highways. They all looked grim, and most were more than we could afford. Finally we looked at an upstairs apartment in a complex called Cole

Manor in Lebanon, near a Toshiba electronics plant. The apartment wasn't much, but we could afford it if I took a break from beauty school and worked a second job during the day.

"What do you think?" BJ asked me as we held hands and walked down the outside flight of steps to the car after looking it over.

"I think it's perfect," I said. "I can't believe we're going to have a place of our own."

I was only a few months removed from having dropped out of high school, and now I was about to move in with a convicted criminal. That's how an adult would describe what I was doing: a choice destined to fail. But to me, it all felt like a romantic adventure that was destined to have a happy ending.

In a strange way, I was right. BJ did lead me to a happy ending because without him, I wouldn't have had Conner. And Conner would create more happiness for me—and for many, many people—than I could have ever possibly imagined. But first, there would be hell to pay. I had no idea how bad my life with BJ was about to turn. The 15% was magic, but the other 85% almost did me in.

chapter eight

A CHOICE

Cayden was diagnosed with spastic cerebral palsy when he was only a few months old. The doctors explained that the disease caused his muscles to tighten, and that was what made it hard for him to control the way he moved. They said he would never be able to walk or talk or take care of himself. As his muscles continued to tighten, they would strain his joints and eventually his heart as his body worked harder to compensate.

One drug they prescribed to help him was a muscle relaxer that eased his pain. A side effect was that it made Cayden get very sleepy very early. Most nights he was in bed as early as 6 o'clock.

As far as Conner knew, this was the way all little brothers behaved, and Conner learned how to spend time with Cayden in the few hours they had together. After school they'd watch TV as they shared a snack. Conner would tell Cayden about his day at school, the lessons he was learning and the things he did at recess. Their different abilities and interests meant that the boys never *played much together. It was rare for them to even be able to eat dessert at the same time because by the time Conner finished his dinner, Cayden would already be fast asleep in bed.*

Conner never liked that Cayden couldn't eat dessert with the rest of us.

"It's not fair," Conner would tell me as I handed out a cookie or a bowl of ice cream.

"I agree," I'd sigh. "But Cayden has his own treats earlier in the day. He just gets tired before the rest of us."

Conner would shrug.

"Still doesn't seem right," he'd say, unsatisfied.

One night after dinner I found Conner climbing a step stool in the kitchen.

"What are you up to?" I asked.

"I'm putting a couple of cookies here to save for Cayden when he wakes up," Conner said, reaching for a cabinet. "He's going to want these later."

"That's a very good idea," I said proudly. "You sure you don't want a cookie now for yourself?"

"No," he said. "I can wait. I'll have mine with Cayden tomorrow."

"O.K.," I said. "Good choice."

———————

SOMETIMES WHEN I look at photographs of the younger me, it's as if I can barely recognize the girl I see there. Of course I know it is me, and I blush at the hairstyles that I thought were cool and the outfits I thought fit me perfectly. Yet I still wonder, What was she thinking? What made her decide to do the things she did? Even the happy pictures give me that feeling.

As I was dragging my stuff out of Donna's house and into my new apartment with BJ, Donna warned me that I was making a big mistake. I thought she just wanted to keep me close to her, like some sort of trophy from her battle with my dad. I didn't consider that she was trying to give me a useful piece of advice. What I wanted was a home of my own. I thought about BJ and me as two people who had been tossed out into the sea, and if we clung to each other tight enough, we'd make a stable life. I thought we'd show everyone that they had underestimated us.

BJ and I didn't have much to fill our apartment on Toshiba Drive, but people stepped up to help. BJ's mom had a friend who was looking to get rid of a big plush sectional from the '80s. It was ugly but free, and we were grateful to have it. My Aunt Susan bought us a little silver and black table with two chairs where we ate. Ashley and her mom came up with a set of pots and pans, and BJ's grandmother took us grocery shopping to fill the empty wooden cabinets in the kitchen.

I had to quit beauty school and get another job so we could afford our new life. I got hired as an assistant manager at Gymboree, where I worked days, and kept my job at Safari's at night. BJ said he was taking as many shifts as he could working construction. With both of us working as hard as we could, we could earn just enough to cover our rent and utilities and go out for dinner one night a week.

We'd been in our new place only a week when, just as my shift was ending at Safari's, Poppy called me to tell me that BJ was back in jail.

"What? What did he do?"

Poppy didn't have answers. She only knew he had been arrested.

I was sure he had violated parole again. The rules were simple and clear. When he wasn't working, BJ was supposed to go straight back to the apartment. I couldn't keep track of him while I was working at night, and I didn't think I had to. I thought he and I were on the same path—the path to building a better life. The truth was BJ hadn't been going straight home after work. He was occasionally slipping out to bars with his buddies, a direct violation of parole. He was always bending the rules until they broke.

The next morning, Poppy and I went to see him in jail. BJ was quiet. He looked at me with puppy-dog eyes.

"Don't worry," he said. "Two weeks. I'll be out of here in two weeks."

"What did you do to get in here?" I asked.

"I violated parole," he said. "I was out having a beer, and I should have gone straight home. I'm sorry, Jenny. It won't happen again."

I was mad, but I wasn't about to give up on the man I loved. He was showing regret. But as I later learned, regret wouldn't stop him from behaving badly again.

"Hang in there," he said to me before I left.

The next two weeks moved slowly. I couldn't take another job, and I didn't think I could do more to support BJ other than stand by him.

The mind fills with all sorts of thoughts when you are sad and by yourself. I questioned whether I was strong enough to "hang in there" for him—but then I would remember how important it was that we believed in each other, trusted each other, no matter what. I had to stay strong and keep my faith, even though I often felt so hopeless and lonely that I thought I might burst.

One night I called my ex-boyfriend Travis. We ended up grabbing a bite together. He must have misread my intentions because he kissed me good night. It was a chaste kiss, and I told Travis that I was fully committed to BJ, but still I felt guilty. I didn't want this hanging over my head.

When BJ was released from jail two weeks later, I was euphoric. I picked him up from the jailhouse, drove straight back to our apartment and practically dragged him up the stairs, drunk from the smell of his Armani cologne and the feel of his touch. We made love and stayed in bed all afternoon.

The next day, I stood at the small stove in our apartment and cracked two eggs.

"I'll start working again, Jenny," BJ said as he watched me. "I'll take as many hours as I can get until my trial."

"When's that?"

"Three or so weeks from now."

"What's going to happen?"

BJ paused.

"They'll probably just extend my probation. I'll have to watch myself better. And I will. I won't get into any more trouble."

As I turned and slid the eggs out of the pan and onto two plates, I knew that this was the moment I had to tell him what had happened with Travis. I knew I'd feel better after I told him the truth.

"BJ, while you were in jail, I had dinner one night with Travis and he kissed me."

BJ's eyes widened.

"That's all that happened. It was nothing, but I had to tell you."

BJ grabbed the plate from my hands and smashed it to the floor.

"I knew I couldn't trust you!" he screamed. "How could you do this to me?!"

I was blown back by how angry he was. My only defense was to get angry right back.

"How dare you say that! I've given up everything in my life because I love you. Nothing happened with Travis. Nothing!"

I had to get away from him in the hope that we'd both cool down. I grabbed my purse and headed for the front door.

"That's right, whore," BJ screamed, even angrier. "Go out into the street where you belong."

He stood up as I laid my hand on the doorknob.

"You gonna go see Travis? Is that where you're going? You whore!"

I opened the door and raced down the stairs. When I looked up from the bottom of the landing, I saw BJ standing at the top of the stairway, waving a can of Coke around in his right hand.

"You're not leaving me!" he screamed. "You're not leaving me!"

Then BJ tilted the Coke can so that drops of soda hit the side of my head and dribbled down my neck. He was laughing at me. I made my way to the car, humiliated. BJ wasn't done, though. He heaved the empty can at my head. I got into my car, my skin and shirt soaked, and tried to stick the key in the ignition while BJ walked up to the car and continued to call me a slut and a whore. As I backed out, I looked back at him standing there. Window shades all around opened as the neighbors tried to get a better view of the spectacle we were making.

I felt so small. I didn't have the words to defend myself, let alone the will. All I could think to do was get away.

chapter nine

RESPONSIBILITY

Children know more than they let on. Just like I knew my mom was sick even though no one wanted to talk to me about it, we never thought Conner was listening to our "grownup" conversations about Cayden and his condition until we heard them replayed to us out of Conner's mouth.

One such conversation was about Cayden's care should anything happen to me or Jeff. Cayden needs constant attention and help—to eat, to keep him calm, to get dressed, even to change the diapers that he has worn since birth and will wear the rest of his life. Who would do that if we weren't around? Who did we trust? Who could bear that responsibility?

"I'll take care of Cayden," Conner called out from the backseat of the car.

I didn't know what to say or how serious he was.

"That's sweet, Conner," I called back. "You're a good brother. But it's a big responsibility."

"It's O.K. I'm good with it."

"What about when you have to go to college or get a job?" Jeff asked.

"That's O.K. We'll go to college together. Live together, too."

It's overwhelming when your 7-year-old talks like that. His intentions were pure, but he was too young to understand. I thought about all the consequences of Conner's feeling the need to care for his brother, and my heart started pounding fast.

I want to make sure Conner gets to live a full life, the kind of life he deserves, and not just a life committed to Cayden. I think about all the things he would miss living like that, and frankly, it makes me afraid to ever die. I never want to leave Conner carrying such a heavy load.

———————

AFTER THE FIGHT with BJ, I drove around, crying. It wasn't just the fight with BJ. It was the realization that I had no place else to go. I'd burned my bridges with my father, and I certainly did not want to go back to Donna's house and prove to her that she was right about BJ and the mistake I was making.

Eventually, I blamed myself for the fight. That's what convinced me that it was right to go back to him. BJ's hearing was coming up soon, and I didn't want to spend the days apart. I had let Travis kiss me. I owned the responsibility for my mistakes and thought it was my duty as a good girlfriend, for our future, to forgive BJ for his anger. After driving around a while, I returned to him to apologize.

BJ's mood had changed. He told me how sorry he was for his angry, humiliating outburst.

"I need you, Jenny," he said as he clung to me. It was exactly what I wanted to hear, exactly what I believed. "You're the only person I can count on, and I love you. I'm sorry. I'm sorry. I'm sorry."

BJ never explained to me what might happen at the hearing, and I never asked. We both calmed down and kept working, trying to put a little money aside in case he had to go back to jail for a week or more. As the day approached for his hearing, I felt sick. I wasn't sleeping great and wasn't eating right. I thought it was just the stress, but as I was driving home from work one night I stopped at the store and bought a pregnancy test.

When I got back to Cole Manor, BJ was getting ready to take a load of laundry down to the washer and dryer. I stopped him.

"BJ, before you go, you know, I've not been feeling right. I thought maybe ... I bought a pregnancy test."

BJ paused at the doorway holding the plastic basket of T-shirts and towels. He looked at me and continued on his way.

As I sat on the toilet for my first pregnancy test, a thousand thoughts flashed through my mind. BJ and the hearing. My father's disapproval if I really was pregnant. Donna too, who had warned me about BJ. I thought about all those Sundays and Wednesdays in church. Of all the sins I had committed, getting pregnant like this felt like the biggest of them all. Would the universe open up and send me straight to hell?

I looked down. There was a sign: positive.

I wasn't looking to have a baby. But—to my surprise—I wasn't scared. In fact, my heart was filled with joy. I was going to be a mother!

Staring at the stick, I imagined my own mother finding out that she was pregnant with Tucker when she was still in high

JENNY LONG WITH BOB DER

school. She wasn't ready to bring a new life into the world, either. But among my friends and family—practically everyone I grew up around—there rarely was a child who came into the world under ideal circumstances. Life just happened, and you made the best of it. I could feel in my soul that I had the power to do as my mom had done—to find a way to just make it work. I also felt strongly that this child was going to bring out the best in me. I had been going down so many bad roads, but a child is an opportunity and reason to change all that. I hadn't been the best person I could be for myself—but I believed I could do it for my baby, and I thought BJ would react the same way.

I was so excited as I walked down to the laundry room to tell BJ the news. But as I stood in the doorway, watching him slide quarters into the machine, I was nervous. There was something about the way he was acting. He knew I was there, but he was ignoring me. The idea of having a baby together wasn't opening him up, it was shutting him down.

"BJ ..."

He didn't respond, so I called out to him again in a louder voice.

"BJ!"

He turned his head and looked at me.

"The test is positive. I'm pregnant!"

I said it with a big grin on my face, but BJ didn't crack a smile. He looked down. I leaned down a little too, trying to catch the expression on his face, but I couldn't see it.

"BJ ... I'm going to have our baby. Aren't you going to say something?"

He reached for the empty laundry basket and walked out the

door without saying a word. As I climbed the steps following him, I was angry at myself for causing his bad mood. I shouldn't have added another burden on him, I thought. He was anxious about his hearing the next day, and I'd dumped this news on him out of nowhere. He didn't need another thing to worry about. I felt like I was doing it all wrong—again.

We ate dinner without speaking, did the dishes side by side in silence and put away the laundry. When it was time for bed, we shut the lights without a word. BJ turned his back to me, his shoulders forming a wall to keep me away. I shut my eyes and pretended to be asleep, but even in the darkness I could feel BJ drifting away.

When the morning came, he got out of bed before I did and got ready for court. I kept looking at him, waiting for the sign that now was the time to talk—a look, a shoulder rub, an embrace, anything—but that sign never came.

In the courthouse, I took a seat in the back next to Poppy and BJ's mom, Lisa. BJ went up front, by the lawyers and the judge. There was a police officer sitting in the front: the man who had been assigned to trail BJ while he was on parole. The state of Tennessee was betting against BJ to make it on the outside— with his long record of parole violations, who could blame it? But it was betting against me, too. It was betting against me for believing in him.

The prosecutor showed a videotape of BJ at a community pool past his curfew. That was an automatic parole violation, and since this was his second one I suspected he might get more than two weeks. But there was more. Next on the stand was the detective who testified that when they brought BJ in for questioning, a drug test found cocaine in his system.

Cocaine.

As that word echoed through the courtroom, I felt like I had just stepped into an elevator shaft and was free-falling. BJ wasn't going back to prison for a few days or even a few weeks. The judge sentenced him to two years.

As I rose from my seat to walk toward the front of the courthouse to speak with BJ, Poppy locked me into a hug. I looked over her shoulder and saw BJ being led away in handcuffs.

I drove back to our apartment in shock. I should have pressed BJ more, questioned the excuses he'd always given me for the times he was late coming home or went out on some errand and didn't get back until 2 a.m. How stupid he must have thought I was for blindly agreeing that things were going to be O.K. Meanwhile he was living with me, lying to me and getting me pregnant.

My "bold life" was a disaster. I thought I was wiser than my years because of all that I had lived through. I believed I had destiny on my side—a miracle waiting for me—something bigger and better than anyone else could see. But I was in a crappy apartment I couldn't afford, holding down two crummy jobs just to stay afloat, I didn't have a high school degree, and I was pregnant by a felon who was going to be in jail when our baby was born.

Suddenly I felt a wave come over me. Strangely, it was a wave of strength. It was time for me to act and make some changes. I'd seen my mom be brave when she was trying to beat cancer, and I knew I had that same strength within me. This baby was my call to action. I would make a better world, or as good a world as I could, for my child. I would eat right, sleep right and go back to get my high school diploma. By the time BJ got out of prison, I'd have it all set up so that we could be a real family, just the three of us. My mind was set, and I had set my mind before, but always on the wrong things. This time I was focused on making a proper life for my baby, and nothing was going to stop me.

chapter ten

CHANGE

When he was about 6 years old, we signed Conner up for organized football, hoping to avoid what had happened with basketball. It was a better experience, for a while. Practices were outside rather than in the gym, and Cayden was more at ease sitting in his chair on the sidelines, soaking up the sunshine and the breeze.

Conner gave it his all every practice—hustling around, listening to the coaches, everything with maximum effort. He was one of the hardest workers on the team, but he was mostly on the bench for game days.

When the season was over, Conner told us that he didn't want to go out for football again.

"It's no fun for me on the sidelines," he explained. "Can't be any fun for Cayden, either."

"Well, sports can be like that," Jeff explained. "You don't always get to play."

"I'd like to find a sport where they let me play," Conner insisted.

"One that Cayden and I can play together."

I was frustrated. I wanted my boys to be happy, but I couldn't figure out how to give them what they wanted. A sport they both could play together—when one boy couldn't even walk? I didn't even know where to begin to fulfill that kind of wish.

———————

I BROKE THE lease on the apartment right away and moved in with BJ's mom. She was happy I was pregnant. She said she was sure that the baby would give BJ extra motivation to straighten up when he was released. I really wanted to believe that myself, but I had doubts. The first call BJ made to me from prison, he told me to "take care" of the pregnancy.

"I spoke to my father," he told me, almost proud. "You call him, and he'll give you some money to take care of it. Don't worry."

"BJ, I wasn't trying to get pregnant, but now that I am, I'm going to have this baby," I said.

BJ turned angry. "If you have that baby, you won't have me," he said.

"Fine," I answered back. "I don't have you now anyway."

BJ must have heard the seriousness in my voice. This time, he gave in first.

"If this is what you want to do, then we'll do it," he told me the next day on the phone. "Just hold down the fort until I get out of here."

For the next nine months, that's exactly what I focused on doing. I went from living with BJ's mom to moving in with his grandmother, a woman we called Mee Maw. I was O.K. with living just about anywhere as long as it was rent-free. I saved my salary to give us a nest egg for when BJ was released. I took good care of myself, slept a lot, ate well and took night classes to get my high school diploma. I didn't have much, but I was going to give my baby the best I could.

I started a new job doing back-office work at a place called Gutter Guard. They installed shields that protected house gutters from falling leaves and twigs. My shift at Gutter Guard was 8 to 5 every day. Then I'd drive from work to evening classes, making up for that failed math credit every night.

On the weekends, you could find me standing in a line at prison—the Charles B. Bass Correctional Complex just outside downtown Nashville. The line started forming as early as 6 a.m. If I got there a little late, like 6:30 or 7, the wait on visiting days would be at least 45 minutes. If it was raining, I was wet. If it was snowing, I was cold. There were mornings when I was so pregnant and worn out that I just wanted to stay in bed and sleep, but BJ needed to know he had a life waiting for him on the other side. Every time he saw me, he saw how much the baby was growing inside me. If that didn't inspire him to change his ways, well, nothing would.

I must have been a sight: this very pregnant lady maneuvering her big belly out of a beat-up car and waddling up to the prison gate. When I finally reached the front of the line, I'd get the same treatment as everyone else: a pat-down from the security guard working the front desk.

Even in prison, BJ kept his sly grin and cocky strut. In fact, he looked more confident and comfortable behind bars. His jeans were starched, and he pressed them himself, so each leg had a hard crease down the front. He kept his hair cut close and his body clean. No bad smells, all soap and water and his favorite Armani Code, which he somehow managed to get from the outside.

When I was just weeks from giving birth, BJ got down on one knee and proposed to me inside that prison. I said yes because I wanted to believe that despite everything, BJ and I could write a happy ending to this ridiculous, trashy fairy tale.

On June 7, 2003, I woke up a bit earlier than I normally would, because it was my wedding day and I needed to make some extra preparations. I put on the big, white belly dress that was to be my wedding gown and got in the passenger seat so my friend Ashley could drive us to prison.

As Ashley turned the steering wheel to the right for the big, swooping curve of Exit 26B, she looked at me somberly.

"Jenny," she said. "Are you sure you want to go through with this?"

I laughed nervously. "Yes, I'm sure."

"No, Jenny. I'm serious. It's not too late. I can turn this car around right now. I'll do it, I swear, all you have to do is tell me."

As far as I was concerned, I was on this ride with BJ, and I intended to see it through to the end. There were many nights when I was alone in bed and my body ached from work and school and the baby so much that I just wanted to give up. I saw these perfect women pictured in the new-mom magazines at the obstetrician's office, and sometimes I resented them.

Then I'd realize that resentment wasn't doing me and my baby much good. I had decided to drop out of school and move in with BJ and to have this baby. I thought about my mom and how she had made a perfect life for us out of a world that didn't have such perfect parts. My baby might have a less-than-perfect beginning, but that didn't mean that we couldn't have a great life. I held on to my vision of how much better everything would be when BJ was released. Then—finally—we'd be a family.

"Keep driving, Ashley. I'm getting married."

My baby was born into a legal family. I was not an unwed mother, and Conner can never be called a bastard child. The day after the wedding, I corrected another mistake: I became a high school graduate.

As I left for the ceremony, I stopped to check myself in the mirror. In my purple cap and gown, I looked like a big round grape that was about to burst. I felt ashamed of myself, but I vowed to never look back with regret, only move forward with determination. I had carried sorrow inside me ever since my mom died, and in many ways that sorrow had never left me. I didn't want my child to be surrounded by that kind of heaviness. My baby deserved a mom who took on the world fresh every day, just as my mother had done. She had always moved forward in life, even if it meant retracing her steps, undoing marriages or dealing with bad choices. I wanted to be the same way. I was changing. It was slow, but I was becoming a better person.

chapter eleven

VIOLENCE

Conner walked off the school bus with his hair a mess and a puffy red lump under his eye.

"What happened?!" I asked as he dropped his backpack on the floor by the door and went to the kitchen. Conner kept walking, pretending everything was normal.

"Your eye! How did that happen?"

Conner just shrugged and turned away. Finally I coaxed the truth out of him: he had gotten into a fight with another child on the bus, one of his friends in the neighborhood who had been to our house many times to play ball and ride bikes. I scolded Conner for getting into a scrape.

"We don't fight to settle disagreements," I said in that stern, motherly voice you don't even know is inside you until you have a child.

"I didn't start a fight," Conner answered quickly.

"Don't sass me," I fired back.

Conner continued to protest. Then he began to tear up. "He started it."

"I don't care who started it. We don't fight."

Conner looked at me with disbelieving eyes.

"You don't know what he said."

This wasn't just about being punished. Something was bothering him.

"What did he say?"

Conner bowed his head.

"What did he say?" I asked in a softer tone.

"He used that word."

"What word?"

"The word. The R word."

I didn't know what Conner was talking about.

"What's the R word?" I finally asked.

Conner couldn't bring himself to spit it out. He was crying harder now. Sobbing.

"It's O.K.," I whispered softly. "Just tell me. I won't get mad, I promise."

Finally, he spoke the word that was causing him so much trouble.

"Retard. He called Cayden a retard. I pushed him, and he punched me in the eye."

MY SON Conner Vance Green was delivered at 8 a.m. on June 28, 2002. Despite being three weeks early, he was a healthy seven and a half pounds. He was pink and pudgy and LOUD, the biggest screamer in the maternity ward.

He was also the most beautiful thing I had ever seen in my life, and I couldn't believe it was possible for me and BJ to have made something so perfect and right.

As I held Conner in my arms, the world felt lighter. Conner's hair was so blond that it looked like thin strands of golden thread. I counted his 10 tiny fingers and 10 tiny toes. Now I understood why my mom had doted on me so much when I was a little girl. A child brings hope into your life.

I felt like Conner and I had already been through so much together. Now he was here in my arms. I didn't know what was going to happen with BJ, or anything else for that matter, but I knew that Conner and I were going to make it together. I was never going to be alone again. I felt complete and safe, and that feeling of safety was not coming from someone else; it was in me. I was the one who chose to bring this life into the world despite the doubts and scowls of others. I was the one who was capable and hardworking. I was connected to this little person—he needed me—and I wanted to be a better person for him. I knew I could be. That feeling made me strong.

Suddenly everything seemed so much clearer—clearer than it had ever been. I'd been operating with a chip on my shoulder from the moment I turned 15, and with a little squeeze from Conner's hand as it wrapped around my finger, that chip fell right to the floor. Bitterness is a terrible motivator. Love is a stronger one.

That night, I slept better than I had in years. The love I had for Conner was unlike any love I had ever felt—it was love without conditions—and I couldn't wait to see what the next new day was going to bring.

Conner was a great-looking baby with expressive brown eyes and an almost perfectly round head. His tiny ears stuck out a little, and his smile radiated like pure joy. I could watch Conner smile for hours. Strangers would ooh and aah at him while we waited in line at the grocery store, and he was a sociable baby. He'd smile at the cooing ladies, and they'd smile back like a reflex they couldn't control.

"He looks just like you!" they'd say.

"You and your husband must be over the moon."

You know how you get to chatting with the grocery-store clerk and the guy at the gas station? Those people I saw almost every week always wanted to know a little more. They'd ask about my husband. How come we never see him come around? What's he do for a living?

At first I was honest. I explained that BJ was in prison. Folks would always wince when they heard that, their chins retreating back and their eyes filling with pity. To me there was nothing worse than that. I never wanted pity, dating back to when I lost my mom. Some people abruptly ended the discussion when they heard my husband was a criminal. They suddenly looked at me like I must be a criminal, too. It takes one to marry one, right? After making that mistake a few times, I started saying he was in construction. Why let prejudice interfere with the affection people naturally expressed when they met my beautiful little boy?

Conner always got the benefit of a clean slate. He was so innocent and unsoiled that as long as I didn't say anything about BJ, I got a good scrubbing just by being around him. I needed that!

I can still picture BJ bouncing Conner on his lap in the prison visiting room. They were both smiling at me, and seeing their heads stacked up one on top of the other, I realized that the person Conner really looked like was BJ.

"Are you ready for some good news?" BJ asked, barely able to control his excitement. Before I could answer he blurted it out.

"I'm getting released early on parole!"

My jaw dropped. I threw my arms around BJ and Conner and squealed like we had just won the lottery. It was a gift to be paroled. It was a fresh start!

"Oh my goodness!" I said over and over. "BJ, that's so terrific. I'm so proud!"

"Now we can really begin living," he said, looking down at Conner.

I couldn't wait to tell my friends and family that BJ was getting out of jail early. It felt like my faith in him was finally being rewarded.

I knew there'd be some rough days of adjustment ahead. I had settled into a routine with Conner. We had our time for naps, our time for dinner and our time for bed. I wasn't sure how BJ was going to adapt to not being able to drop everything on a whim to hit the town. My priorities were different, and I thought BJ would fall in line, too. But I wasn't as blindly certain as I used to be. I knew family life wasn't going to be easy for him.

Conner was a little more than 3 months old when BJ got out of prison. As we drove back to Mee Maw's, BJ kept looking back to Conner in the car seat, not focusing on the road ahead. I could see it in BJ's face—he wasn't just excited, he was absolutely wired.

"What do you want to do?" I asked BJ as the prison building got smaller and smaller in our rearview mirror.

We looked at each other and smiled. BJ was back in control of his life, and he didn't need any parole board or security guard to tell him what he could do as long as he stayed out of trouble.

"Let's go back home and rest a bit," I said, slipping my husband a sly look. "Then maybe we can take you shopping."

BJ looked at me cautiously.

"Don't worry, we can afford it," I said. "I've been saving up to get you new shoes, at least. Conner and I don't want you walking around in those jail shoes anymore."

BJ just smiled. It was shaping up to be one of the happiest days either of us had had in a long time.

The Hickory Hollow Mall was pretty empty and a bit run-down, but it had what we needed. We focused first on finding BJ some comfortable work boots for the construction job he was about to start and something else with a little style for just walking around. BJ and I took turns pushing Conner in his stroller, and we both beamed with pride whenever someone glanced inside and cooed at our little boy.

BJ found the work boots pretty quickly. We strolled the mall, taking our time. I spotted an Express. I had lost some of my pregnancy weight and wanted to find a good pair of dark pants for work.

"Let's pop in here."

BJ stood over the stroller at the end of the clothes rack while I looked for something good. As I worked my way down the row, I heard my cell phone ring and grabbed it.

"Travis, hi!" I said with genuine surprise. "Haven't heard from you in a while."

I looked up and saw a wave of rage overcome BJ's body. His neck veins bulged and his jaw clenched as his eyes widened. He went from having a great time to looking like he was about ready to kill me.

"You bitch! I knew you were a whore, I knew it!"

BJ lunged forward and grabbed the phone out of my hand. People in the store looked up with shock and fear.

"I can't believe you did this, you whore! You did this to me again!"

BJ grabbed the phone from my hand and swung it fast and hard, hitting me across the right side of my face.

"You cheated on me, you whore!"

I hadn't spoken to Travis since that desperate, lonely dinner so many months before, but BJ was raging so hard there was no time to explain anything. I just needed to leave the store to get away from the humiliation.

I got my hands on the stroller and headed for the exit. BJ followed, yelling at me the whole way. I wanted to disappear.

As I reached our car, I started to explain that I had no idea why Travis had called me. I thought maybe he would calm down—even just a little—now that we were outside. But BJ wouldn't give me a moment to say anything. He was wound up and furious, his arms waving around as he got more and more belligerent. He hit me again—lowering his fist onto my head—and I screamed. We were making so much noise that a woman came over and asked me if everything was all right.

Seeing that woman stopped BJ from hitting me. I guess he realized that if he didn't stop, this woman would call the police and he'd be back in jail the same day he got out.

BJ shoved the stroller at me and ran off. All I could think about was making sure Conner was safe—he was, resting angelically in his stroller. I had no idea where BJ was now. And, frankly, I didn't care. This wasn't my husband. This was a monster.

I strapped Conner into his car seat and folded up the stroller. I wasn't safe to drive and I knew it, but I had to get out of the parking lot before he found me again. When I got to Mee Maw's house and looked in my purse, I realized he'd lifted all the money out of my wallet, the whole $200 that I'd saved to buy him clothes and new shoes.

I needed to sleep. I knew I could depend on Mee Maw to take care of Conner while I got my brain back inside my head. But before I could rest, I wanted to know that we were safe. I called around to BJ's family and found out he had called Ashley from a bar. Honestly, I couldn't stop to care what he was thinking. I just needed to know he wasn't anywhere near us.

I put Conner down in his bed, right next to mine in the bedroom. Moms always sleep with one ear cocked to hear if the baby needs them, so BJ must have been sneaking quietly when he entered our bedroom the next morning at 6 a.m., reeking of alcohol. I woke up and he was on top of me, his hands around my neck, whispering to me, "I'm gonna kill you. I'm gonna kill you."

I started screaming and kicking. Conner woke up and started crying, too, from the commotion. Mee Maw came running down the hallway and burst into the room.

"BJ, YOU GET YOUR HANDS OFF OF HER RIGHT NOW!"

BJ didn't listen to many women, but he respected Mee Maw. The minute he heard her voice, he let go of my neck.

The next half hour felt like a day and a half. Everything took place in slow motion. The silence and tension were unbearable. BJ took Conner out of his bed. I watched him closely, and all my mom alarms started going off—what was he going to do with the baby?—but holding Conner actually calmed him down. He was trying to soothe our son to stop his crying. BJ carried Conner down the hallway to the kitchen, leaving me alone in the room.

I realized once and for all that not only was this never going to be a family—this was no way to live. I could never trust BJ again. Conner and I had to get away before he killed me. All those people who told me stories about how violent and unreliable he was were right. He belonged in prison. He was most comfortable there. My son and I were going to have to make a life of our own. But how could I get us away from him?

I went into the kitchen, where BJ was feeding Conner. He looked at Conner with such love and tenderness, but when his eyes strayed up to me, the look was of pure hatred. I was chilled by it, and I feared what would happen when Mee Maw left for work and Conner went down for his morning nap.

If I grabbed Conner and left the house, BJ would know I was leaving him forever—leaving with his son—and I feared that he would start beating me again to stop me.

I decided to do things another way—really, the only way I could think of. I said I needed to get a little air and I was going to drive down to the store. Did they need anything? Then I got in my car and headed straight to the gas station to call someone for help—someone I could trust and count on. To my surprise, the only person that came to mind was the person I had spent so much of my life trying to avoid: my father.

chapter twelve

PEACE

Cayden has always loved bath time. It's a chore to get him in the tub, his body a long tangle of arms and legs that fight you when you need him to bend and move. His feet always bang against the door frame when I carry him in, but it's either his feet or his head so I'll take the feet. Besides, he doesn't seem to mind the wrestling once he's lying back in the warm water. You can feel the tension release from his body. He relaxes.

Cayden's favorite part is when I wash his hair. My hands rub in the shampoo, and his lips melt into a gentle smile. Then comes the best moment, the warm water running over his face to rinse away the suds. He loves the feeling of the running water. He absolutely loves it. Watching how much he appreciates such a small pleasure reminds me of what really matters in life.

Cayden has stress and upsets in his life—we all do—but when he's in the water he finds peace.

DAD'S NUMBER WAS the only one that came into my head, but I didn't want to dial it. My hands were trembling.

"Hello?"

"Dad, it's me. I need you. BJ's gone crazy. He's hitting me and talking about killing me. I woke up this morning with his hands around my neck choking me."

"Where are you?" His voice was direct and urgent.

"I'm at a gas station. He's back at his grandmother's house."

"Where's Conner?"

"He's safe. But BJ's grandmother is probably going to leave for work soon and … I need help. I need to get us out of that house. We have to get away."

There was a pause.

"Give me the address. Wait 15 minutes, then go back to get Conner."

"O.K."

I hung up the phone. Then I cried. I just disintegrated. I had left my baby behind with that maniac who wanted to kill me. How did I know he wasn't hurting Conner? I felt in my heart that he would never harm his own boy—but I didn't know for sure. I realized as I counted down the minutes that I had no idea what he was capable of doing.

When I left, BJ seemed calm, but I knew his rage toward me was still simmering beneath the surface. What if he decided the best way to get to me was to harm Conner—or to take him who knows where? Suddenly I was panic-stricken. What if I had chosen wrong? What kind of mother leaves her child behind? Was Conner safe? Where was he?

Exactly 15 minutes later I peeled out of the gas-station parking lot and sped over to Mee Maw's. When I pulled up, two police officers were dragging BJ down the walkway, his hands cuffed behind his back. He was almost at the squad car when he saw me.

"Whore! I see you there, bitch! You cheated on me!"

The police lowered BJ into the car, and he started kicking at the windows. All I could see were the heels of his new work boots stomping on the glass.

The police drove away, and I waited another minute before I got out of my own car, shaking. Jenny, you have *totally* screwed everything up, I thought to myself, trying to catch my breath. Then I went inside to find Conner, who was safe and unharmed in his grandmother's arms. I broke down again—relieved but completely overwhelmed by everything that had happened.

When I first dropped out of school, I thought I was a badass who had everything figured out. My cocky attitude, my confidence that the world was mine if I just acted bold enough, that was all a front. Now it was time for me to grow up for real.

In the days after BJ went back to prison, I thought hard about the mess I had made of my life. It wasn't all my fault, but a lot of it was. Why had I been so attracted to a man like BJ, a man who wore danger like a cheap T-shirt? I came to realize that the attention BJ gave me was blinding. I had craved that kind of attention ever since my mother died, and BJ used my blind spot to hide his flaws. If it hadn't been BJ, it would have been someone just like him. The sad truth was if you put me in a room with a hundred eligible men, the one I would have ended up with would walk and talk just like BJ Green.

I took my last trip to prison to serve the divorce papers.

I gave a lot of thought to what I was going to say to BJ when I threw those papers on the table. I pictured myself unleashing all my pent-up anger and resentment, backed by the safety of the prison guards. But when the moment finally arrived, BJ didn't seem worth all that speechifying. I just slipped the papers across the table.

"Sign these and we're done."

BJ must have been expecting it, because he didn't even glance at the forms. All he said was that he wanted custody of Conner.

I wasn't going to let that happen. BJ and I were done as a family. Besides, the walls of prison suited BJ a whole lot better than family life. As he had proven many times before, he couldn't make it outside a cell block—at least not for very long.

Conner and I found a place to live—a place away from BJ. We moved into an apartment with Ashley. She and I split the chores and expenses and even worked together at Gutter Guard. Our life wasn't exciting or glamorous, but it was stable and dependable. That was a step in the right direction.

I wanted nothing to do with men for a while, probably because I wasn't ready to trust my judgment. Besides, my mother raised me by herself, and I believed that I could do the same thing for Conner. I was happy being alone, but even though I wasn't looking to find a father figure for Conner, one did emerge: a co-worker at Gutter Guard, a quiet man named Jeff Long.

Jeff was like the country boy next door, a country boy who rarely said more than three words at a time. Whenever I was around him, seeing him in the office or even just saying good morning, he'd nod and look away. Sometimes he'd mumble. He almost never looked me in the eye.

"What's the deal with that guy, Jeff?" I asked Ashley one night while we were sitting on the couch watching TV with Conner. "Why doesn't he talk?"

"He's just quiet," Ashley answered. "Can't a guy be quiet?"

That was a really good question. I had never been around a guy like Jeff.

One day I was helping a bunch of the installers load the work van. It was the usual scene. The guys were good-natured but rowdy because there were only two women in the office. It was summertime, and I wore my Gutter Guard shirt over a pair of khaki shorts with my hair tied into pigtails. We were all busy loading boxes into the van, but there was a good bit of small talk to make the time pass easier.

"You guys have something fun planned for the weekend?" I asked.

"Not unless you've got something planned for us!" one of the installers yelled back, and they all started to snicker like schoolboys.

I just smiled and let it go.

"What about you, Jeff?"

He looked startled, like a kid who hadn't done any of the homework being called out in front of the class.

"You got weekend plans, Jeff?"

His face turned bright red, and he didn't know where to look.

"No," he finally mumbled. "I'm good."

The other guys doubled over with laughter.

Over the next several months I got to know Jeff well, first as a co-worker and then as a friend. He lived with his grandparents all the way out in Jackson County, in the small town of Gainesboro. The drive from Gainesboro to our office was at least an hour and a half each way, but I never heard Jeff complain about it, and he was never late.

Turned out that Jeff Long did talk if he knew he could trust you. And once he started talking, he didn't hold anything back.

— *chapter thirteen* —

RESPECT

When people first meet Cayden, they find it hard to read his thoughts or emotions. He rarely looks at strangers, even if they are speaking to him directly. He's easily distracted, whooping and screeching at unpredictable times, and that can be uncomfortable for someone who isn't used to it. After a while, most people start ignoring Cayden, acting like he isn't in the room or can't hear or understand what they're saying.

It's obviously different for those of us in the family. We can tell when Cayden likes something and when he doesn't. He'll clap his hands and smile when he's excited.

"Cayden, want to go to the YMCA?"

He'll clap because he loves to go to the YMCA. He goes to the Youth Room, where he gets to be around other kids. Cayden loves to be part of the action.

Conner tells me that Cayden has a girlfriend at the YMCA. She's about the same age, and Cayden likes to play with her hair. Conner teases his brother about that.

The kids sometimes don't know what to do around Cayden, so Conner always hangs out with his brother. Conner likes to play basketball, and while he shoots, Cayden rolls around the court in his wheelchair. Conner also helps out if Cayden has a breakdown. Anything can trigger a sudden outburst, even boredom. Conner can usually calm his brother, but sometimes he can't. Sometimes I can't calm him down, either. But Cayden knows we're there for him. Sometimes that's the best you can do for someone. Just be there.

———————

JEFF LONG TOLD me a lot about his childhood, how every day he witnessed the fight between peace and volatility, or as he called them, "Dad" and "Mom." Jeff's dad was the calm one: quiet and churchgoing. He was the kind of man Jeff modeled himself after: a simple country boy who never met a problem that couldn't be worked out holding a fishing pole. Jeff's mom was a firecracker with a fuse about as long as an inchworm. She came from a family of drinkers who loved good times and good fights. Usually, those fights were with Jeff's dad, but as Jeff and his brother got older, they became the targets of her anger, too. She got mad when they horsed around, or didn't listen right away, or just reminded her too much of their father.

Jeff didn't like drama or hostility. When his parents split up he chose to go with his dad and moved in with his paternal grandparents in Gainesboro. Jeff went to church every Sunday and fished or hunted with his dad and grandfather during the week. Their world was simple—work hard, take care of your family, thank God for your blessings and fear Him when you had sinned.

Jeff soaked up those lessons. But staying on the path of good wasn't always easy. Temptation found Jeff. In high school he started partying with friends to dull the boredom of small-town life, and that led to pills. He also began dating a girl who was wilder than him, more adventuresome. She was his BJ. One night in Gainesboro, Jeff and his girlfriend were caught breaking into cars. Jeff had been making drug deals for people—as a favor to them—but if they left him on the hook with the real dealers, he thought it was only fair to break into their car and take a radio to pay back the money they owed. Jeff was arrested and sentenced to a year in prison.

Jeff cried when he faced his grandparents after his sentencing. He knew he had let them down, but he was most upset because he was disappointed in himself.

Jeff served his prison time like a man and hated every minute of it. He vowed to get out and never return. That's why he made the hour-and-a-half drive from Gainesboro. He was being good, sticking close to his grandparents and the life he knew was right.

After all I had been through with BJ, I was cautious about opening my heart to Jeff. I could tell he was a gentler man, a more sincere man, than my ex. But he had a past, too. I didn't want to risk getting too attached, and I didn't want to bring new danger anywhere near Conner.

My feelings started to change the first time I saw Jeff and Conner together. Jeff was over at my apartment, sitting on the sofa and holding Conner's hands as he tried to stand. Conner's legs were wobbly, and Jeff was slowly pulling him up a little bit at a time and then letting go, trying to get Conner to balance and hold more of his weight each time.

"You can do it, Little Man. You got this," Jeff kept saying.

They both were smiling, and I felt the hairs on the back of my neck tingle. They were beaming at each other, and Conner was laughing that big belly laugh he had when he was really loving the moment. He was getting stronger with Jeff around. Maybe I could get stronger by being around him, too. I had been burned by BJ, but I allowed myself to be open—cautiously—to that kind of hope.

The three of us started spending a lot of time together. I even let Jeff stay at my apartment so he could avoid the long drives back and forth to his grandparents' place. He was always a gentleman around me and Conner, and it took a while before our relationship became a romantic one.

I was attracted to Jeff. But I was in no rush to have our relationship get too serious. Technically, I was still married to BJ, waiting for him to finally sign those divorce papers.

Eventually I fell in love with Jeff in a romantic way. Jeff was a good man, a decent man, a man who strove to do the right things. He had made mistakes, but unlike BJ he had learned from those mistakes and changed his ways. Jeff had the strength of character to make that kind of commitment.

As time passed, Jeff and I decided to move into a place of our own together. We didn't commit to marriage or anything more. We just decided to take one small step at a time.

Jeff really thrived trying to make a more stable life for us. The responsibility gave him purpose, a reason to stretch and be more ambitious. Jeff decided to quit his job at Gutter Guard and began apprenticing with his uncle to become an electrician. He said it was going to take a lot of work and some long hours, but it would be worth it because he could make more money once he was established in a real trade.

Being around Jeff, I realized he wasn't the type to jolt me like a lightning bolt. I felt something much calmer with Jeff; I felt comfortable. And it was uncomfortable for me to feel comfortable. I was constantly on alert for a sign that the feeling was wrong or about to end. It's pretty messed up to admit that about myself, but it's the truth. I was a damaged person trying to get better.

Just as Conner and I were moving forward in our life with Jeff, BJ walked back in. He had finally finished his sentence and was released from prison. He called me to ask about Conner.

"Is he growing big and strong, Jenny? Does he know about me? God, I wish I could see him."

The sound of his voice shot through my body. The more he talked, the more uncomfortable I felt. This man was poison to me.

Still, I felt I should let him see Conner. He was my son's biological father. I thought about my own mother and how she never completely shut my father out of my life. She sent him pictures of me at the holidays. She tried to get me to talk to him on the phone. She was always looking for ways to remind him that he had created something good in this world. It must have had an impact on him, because my father did step up to take care of me after she died. As much as I had issues with my dad, I knew that he loved me and I was grateful for his efforts to protect me, even if I usually worked against him.

I also thought I owed something to Conner. I owed him the chance to have some relationship with his father. I didn't want him to grow up and learn that I had kept him away. As long as BJ wasn't a danger to our son, I was willing to see if they could build a bond. Perhaps, given time, Conner could change BJ in ways that I never could. Maybe he would make BJ a better person, the type of person he always talked about wanting to become.

It wasn't meant to be. Just a few days after that phone call, BJ was at a bar about a mile from where he was living. He was getting ready to leave when he saw a friend standing next to a low-slung, red Japanese motorcycle. BJ loved bikes, and he asked his buddy if he could take it for a ride even though it had been raining and BJ had been drinking. His friend agreed. BJ roared out into the suburban streets, weaving his way around the curves of pavement and little stretches of open country road. Witnesses heard him downshifting as he came around a curve, followed by a skid.

BJ was thrown from the bike and hit his head against a thick concrete drainage pipe. He was wearing a helmet, but his injuries were so severe, he had to be airlifted to the hospital—Vanderbilt Hospital, the same place my mother had died.

After the accident, I was asked to go to Vanderbilt, too. Technically, I was still BJ's wife.

When I arrived the doctor started asking me about how to care for BJ. Should they keep him on life support? He was in a coma with only a slim chance to recover. I explained the situation and said BJ's family should be the ones to make the decisions. It wasn't my place anymore. But I did want to see him. If this was going to be goodbye, I wanted to say my piece.

The doctor escorted me to the room where BJ was clinging to life. I could hardly recognize the man who lay in the middle of a tangle of tubes. His head was puffy and bloated. He must have been burning up inside because I could feel the heat just standing near him.

I leaned in and whispered in his ear.

"BJ, it's me."

There was no reaction. I felt so sad: mostly for BJ and his family and for Conner, who would never know his dad. My dad was a troubled young man, but he had redeemed himself with me later in life. BJ would never have that chance. The only words I could come up with to say to him were "I'm sorry."

I was sorry—sorry for the way everything had turned out. I believe BJ loved me. He just had more hurt in him than he had love to share. I also believe he wanted to change his life for the better—he just didn't know how.

The next day BJ was in surgery for 13 hours, but his condition didn't improve. He lived a few more days on life support before passing away on November 4, 2004—my 21st birthday.

I brought Conner to see BJ at the visitation before his funeral service. He'll probably never remember being there, and he doesn't seem to remember BJ at all as the years have passed. But it was important to me to take him. One day I'll be able to explain to Conner that he paid final respects to his father. I never want him to carry any guilt that he wasn't there.

chapter fourteen

FAMILY

I have always told Conner and Cayden that family should be a special bond. It's easy to enjoy the good times, but you get to know and appreciate what you really have when times are tough.

If their relationship is ever tested, I want my boys to be there for each other. I don't care what their differences are. I don't care if they disagree or bump heads. At the end of the day, I want them to always stick together and help each other out. That's the kind of bond I want my boys to share.

I know my boys share that kind of love. I see it in the way they treat one another. They appreciate and respect each other. They help each other out—Conner in ways that are more obvious and Cayden in ways that are more subtle. But Conner knows he can count on Cayden. He can always count on him to be his loving brother.

JEFF'S TRANSITION TO becoming an electrician was tough for all of us. We had moved into a small place in Cookeville, farther from Nashville but closer to Jeff's uncle, who was training him. Jeff was putting in long hours without much pay, and I was switching among jobs to try to make up the difference. I couldn't land a serious career job even though I tried, and I needed flexible hours to take care of Conner. So I took any work I could find that paid a little something and fit our needs. I worked for a bank call center, even behind the counter at a Dairy Queen.

A lot of nights, the stress left Jeff and me with short fuses. Jeff would escape to his fishing to calm down. I didn't have the same kind of outlet, so sometimes I just stewed. When it all got to be too much, I would pick stupid fights with Jeff—turning small annoyances into big issues. I wasn't proud of my behavior, but I needed to let off steam.

Conner was the glue that kept us together. He just had a way about him. He was such a happy little boy, and he wanted us to be happy, too. We did our best to live up to his expectations.

Conner had started calling Jeff "Daddy," and it made me a little nervous. I didn't want Jeff to freak out and feel any added pressure. One night I asked him about it.

"It doesn't bother me," Jeff said.

I was relieved, so I asked the natural next question: "How does it make you feel?"

Jeff smiled. "It makes me feel like I'm his dad."

Soon we found out that Jeff was going to be a dad to a child of our own. I was pregnant. Of course, I was worried. We weren't in the best situation to welcome another child. We were living on ramen noodles and boxed mashed potatoes until Jeff could start making steady money as a full-time electrician rather than scraping by as an apprentice. I wanted to be happy about being pregnant again, but mostly I was nervous—about money, my future with Jeff, everything.

Jeff's emotions were hard to read. He was always so tight-lipped when it came to his feelings. He wasn't cold, as BJ had been when I told him I was pregnant with Conner, but I could tell he was anxious. I didn't blame him. I felt the strain, too.

The morning after I told Jeff the news, we woke up in blood-soaked sheets. I shook Jeff awake, and we raced to the hospital. Jeff didn't know what to do. Maybe he was scared or just overwhelmed, but he couldn't bring himself to come into the emergency room with me. He stayed waiting in the car while I made my way inside the hospital to find out what was wrong.

It didn't take long for the doctors to tell me that I had lost the baby. The fetus was only a few weeks old, and we weren't trying to have a child, but I felt deep sadness, and so alone. I was hurting physically and emotionally, and I wanted my man holding my hand. When I got to the car and told Jeff what had happened, he didn't explain what he was feeling, but I could tell he was shaken. I wish we had been able to comfort each other through the loss, but we were on separate islands of grief.

There was heaviness between us after the miscarriage. I wanted to talk about my emotions, but he turned silent. I guess that was his defense, or maybe just his nature. I should have forced the issue, but instead I just buried it too, hoping the hurt would ease over time.

The miscarriage left me fertile, and I was pregnant within a month. We weren't trying to get pregnant again, but we did. Maybe it was because of the miscarriage, but this time Jeff seemed immediately happy with the news that we were going to have another child. I was happy, too—happy to see Jeff so excited and happy for a break from the sadness. Jeff and I were celebrating, cautiously but with great joy.

We told Conner the news, and he was practically jumping up and down.

"It's gonna be a boy!" he declared.

"We don't know yet," I said.

"Yeah, but I know it is," he said firmly. "I'm getting a brother!"

"Well, if you do, you're gonna have to teach him how to fish," Jeff chimed in.

"I'll teach him all about fishing," Conner said confidently. "I'll show him how to do a whole lot of things."

Physically, I felt very much the same as I had with Conner, only a bit more tired and a lot less anxious since I knew what to expect.

As the pregnancy developed, I started believing Conner might be right that I would be bringing another little boy into the world. One day as I was walking through the drugstore, I saw a framed picture of two brothers, one just a few years older than the other, sitting side by side as they fished at a lake. They sat so close together, you just knew that they were each other's best friend. The picture brought a tear to my eye, and I bought it and hung it in the nursery. That was going to be Conner and his little brother one day. I looked at that picture all the time to remind myself of what family meant and what our future was going to look like. I couldn't wait until we could take down the frame and replace the photo with a real one of our two boys.

Jeff and I still weren't talking about marriage, but to me we were a family already. The pregnancy just cemented it. The last hurdle was sharing the news of my pregnancy with my father. I call it a hurdle because even though I had gradually drawn my dad back into my life after the heroic way he rescued me from BJ, I still feared his judgment. I decided to tell him the news in a letter. If I told him face to face or on the phone, I knew I'd get flustered. In a letter, he'd have to read my feelings straight through before he could say anything. It would work better that way, better for me at least.

I sat down at the kitchen table, spread out the writing paper and took the cap off my pen. I didn't know how to start. *Dear Dad, I'm pregnant.* No, it would be better to start off with something affectionate. *Dear Dad, You know how much I love you and depend on you.* That sounded phony, because it wasn't true and my father knew it. If I really depended on him, I wouldn't have waited until I was four months pregnant to tell him I was having another baby. Finally, I settled on the message I wanted to send.

Dear Dad,

It's been a while since we spoke so I decided to write to you to give you big news. You're going to be a granddaddy again! I know what you're thinking, Dad. You're thinking this isn't a great time for me and Jeff to add to our family. But life surprises you. Sometimes those surprises turn out great. I think this is a happy surprise, and I hope you will too once you get used to the idea.

You may think Jeff and I are taking on too much. But we don't think so. Jeff really is Conner's dad now and he and I have learned so much about raising kids. We've also learned a lot about each other. Jeff is different from BJ. He's a better man. I think we're going to be great parents for this child. I know I'm much better prepared to be a mom.

Try not to worry. I'm not worried, except about one

thing: Is it possible to love another baby as much as I love Conner? It seems impossible because I love him with my whole heart. Maybe, with this second baby, my heart will grow.
I love you Dad,
Jenny

I mailed that letter filled with hope. Being with Jeff and knowing I could depend on him to be a good father was making me stronger. I would never have handled this announcement so well before Jeff came along. Yes, we had our fights and sometimes we disappointed each other, but at the moment when I was sending off that letter to my dad, I felt great about my family and our future. We faced some strong headwinds, but we were making our way forward.

— chapter fifteen —

UNITED

Mornings in our house are probably like they are for most families: routine. I wake up before 5 to pack lunches for the boys. Cayden carries a lunch box decorated with monsters. Conner has a plain blue one—he doesn't want any cartoon characters now that he's older.

The boys usually have about a half hour together for breakfast before their buses arrive. Conner likes Pop-Tarts. Cayden loves Froot Loops. He insists on them. Sometimes he'll tuck them into his lap to save for the ride to school.

With the TV blaring behind him, Conner does all the talking, of course. He'll tell his brother about what's going to happen that day at school, and he loves jokes. Sometimes he saves one for the morning so he can tell Cayden a new one at breakfast. Cayden will react like most little brothers—sometimes he'll clap with approval and other times he won't pay much attention, especially if there's something more interesting on the TV.

It's not exciting or eventful, but it's more steady and predictable than the afternoons when Conner has homework or sports and Cayden has a doctor's appointment. It's less than an hour of time. Not much, really. But it always ends the same way. Conner reaches out with both arms before his brother wheels out the door to catch his bus. "Come and give your Bubba a hug," he says before sending his brother on his way.

———————

CAYDEN WAS BORN on October 10, 2005, by scheduled C-section. The night before my surgery, Jeff and I cleaned my car for the ride to the hospital. It was a clear, beautiful evening, and I imagined what nights like this would be like when my boys were old enough to run around together and ride their bikes through the neighborhood.

Everything about that night felt peaceful and good. Jeff was about to be promoted from apprentice to full-time electrician. I was feeling less restless, more comfortable in my responsibilities. I had gradually become settled into my relationship with Jeff. We'd been together for three years, and we'd made it. We had a beautiful son in Conner, and our new baby would just bring us more joy. I was so happy to have our feet on the ground and a plan for the future. I sometimes thought back to that crazy afternoon at the mall with BJ as a turning point for me, for my family. Now I was thinking about my choices rather than just acting out of impulse—and that helped me see light up ahead after years of darkness.

"I think we're ready," Jeff said as he finished rubbing down the car.

"Yeah," I said. "We're ready."

The C-section went smoothly. Cayden came out calm and sweet, more like Jeff because he has such a quiet disposition. I held him in my arms and checked all the things a mother does when she meets her new baby—10 fingers and 10 toes, clear blue eyes—he was perfect. About the only problem that first day was that I didn't get to spend as much time as I wanted with him. His breathing was irregular, so the doctors had him hooked up to a machine until his lungs were strong enough so he could breathe on his own.

"Your son is going to be just fine," the nurse assured me. "This is not uncommon."

Cayden's breathing never did get regular enough for them to bring him back to me in my hospital room. When I felt strong enough from my C-section recovery, I went to see him in the neonatal ICU. Seeing him there was quite a shock. He had a helmet strapped around his head that bathed him in oxygen because newborns can't really handle a ventilator. It was hard to see our baby like that. He looked so skinny and alone in the incubator. I trusted the doctors when they said it would be only for a day, and sure enough, the day after I left the hospital we were back to bring Cayden home.

Right away it was clear that Cayden was different from Conner. Conner was always alert and restless, hard to get to sleep. He had colic and stomach trouble that kept him up screaming much of the night. Cayden slept all the time. I even had to wake him up to feed him.

At first, I felt blessed that I was able to get some good rest. But after a while I started to worry a little. Maybe Cayden was sleeping too much. I called the pediatrician's office to ask if this could be a symptom of something wrong, but the nurse just laughed and told me not to worry.

"Some newborn babies sleep a lot!" she said cheerfully. "Consider yourself lucky."

I did consider myself lucky, but I still worried.

Conner hit all his milestones on time. Every time we went to the pediatrician, he was right where he should be. I had the same expectations for Cayden, but when he was little more than a month old I noticed that something basic was off. Around 6 weeks is when you can tell from the tiny movements of their eyes and heads that babies have figured out how to recognize one person from another—or at least they know how to recognize who's Mom and who isn't. Cayden didn't do that. His eyes didn't seem to focus on anything. His left one turned in a bit, and both of them seemed to scan the ceiling.

I would sit with Cayden during those moments when he was awake to watch his eyes as they moved rhythmically back and forth, with that one lazy eye moving hardly at all. I tried not to work myself up too much. I kept telling myself it was one of those things that would correct itself as he grew older. Or maybe he'd have to wear glasses or have an operation to bring his eyes in focus.

I planned to bring it up at his next doctor's checkup, but in the meantime I asked Jeff to look at Cayden's eyes, too. Was he seeing what I was seeing?

"Yeah, you're right," Jeff said. "He seems a little cross-eyed."

"I had a lazy eye when I was a little girl, but I grew out of it," I said. "It might be something that I passed on to Cayden. Sorry, baby."

Jeff and I were both eager for Cayden's two-month checkup.

We wanted to get confirmation that everything was O.K. Jeff took some time off work so he could sit with Conner in the cheerful waiting room filled with toys and kids, while I went into one of the examination rooms with Cayden.

I watched the nurse entering his height and weight onto his chart as she cooed over my little boy and I beamed back, chattering about what a good sleeper he was. The nurse just kept nodding and measuring Cayden's head. Then she left to get the doctor. There was something about the way she left the room—something sudden, something urgent.

I texted Jeff, "The doctor is about to check out Cayden." About a minute later, Jeff came through the door with Conner. The doctor stood at his desk scanning Cayden's chart before reaching into his pocket to pull out a tape measure. He measured Cayden's head himself before staring into his eyes.

"We've been thinking that Cayden's eyes are a little crossed. Do you think so?" I asked. "I had a lazy eye myself when I was little. It was my left one …"

The doctor didn't answer. He started to check Cayden's reflexes, moving his legs back and forth and paying attention to his hips. Then he held him and bounced him on his lap, like he was on a little trampoline.

"I've also noticed that his legs seem real strong. He can lock up his knees really tight …" I was babbling, but I wanted to get the doctor to tell us something. I wanted him to speak, and all the chatter was my attempt to get him to say something about what he saw in Cayden. His silence was making me nervous.

The doctor scribbled some notes on Cayden's chart. When he was done, he patted Cayden on the head and flashed a slight smile.

"You can get him dressed again," the doctor said. Then he left the room. A few minutes later, the doctor returned.

"There are things we saw today that we need to explore further," he said. "The first thing is Cayden's head is smaller than it should be at his age."

"What does that mean?" I asked.

"It could mean a variety of things. You are right about his eyes crossing, but the pupils also quiver a bit, and he doesn't seem to be able to focus his gaze."

"Do you think he needs glasses?" I asked.

"Glasses are for treating an eye problem. I want to find out what's causing the eye problem. We're going to schedule an MRI to scan his brain."

That didn't sound good.

"O.K. What do you think might be wrong?"

"Try not to worry. We'll be able to answer your questions more completely after the MRI."

"I understand, but what do you think might be wrong?"

I looked over at Jeff. He was as concerned as I was.

"The eye fluttering and inability to focus is called a nystagmus, a sign of pressure on the brain. That's usually a sign that something is wrong neurologically. It could be a tumor. That's why I'm scheduling the MRI. I want to make sure."

Jeff and I drove home in silence, with Conner and Cayden both asleep in their car seats. My mind bounced like a rubber ball from one thought to another. A tumor. My little boy, only 6 weeks old, and he might need to have brain surgery? The doctor didn't want to scare us, but my imagination was running wild.

"Oh my God, Jeff," I finally said when we were nearing home. "Do you think Cayden has a brain tumor?"

MOM AND ME
We didn't have a lot of money, but my mother made sure my childhood was filled with love and special memories.

MAGICAL
Growing up in Old Hickory was comforting, happy and exciting. I didn't think life could be any better.

GROWING UP FAST My father and mother *(top, with my half brother Tucker)* split not long after I was born. My dad took me in after my mom died, and in six short years I would become a fast-living teen and pregnant high school dropout.

NOT THE WAY I PICTURED IT

I lived with various members of BJ's family through my pregnancy, including his grandmother. I finally returned to night classes to earn my diploma, graduating days before I gave birth to Conner.

NOT MEANT TO BE

With BJ in prison for most of my pregnancy and Conner's infancy, the three of us spent only a few hours together as a family.

FINALLY, FAMILY
Jeff was so different from BJ: a good man who instantly became Conner's true dad. When we had Cayden together, there was never a doubt that we would raise him despite his CP and the hard road ahead.

MY MIRACLES
Conner never treated Cayden any differently because of his condition. He always accepted him and cherished him as his loving brother.

READY OR NOT
When they started competing together in triathlons, the only swim stroke Conner knew was the dog paddle.

NO DISTANCE TOO FAR
Cayden will never be able to walk or talk, but he is as much a part of the team as Conner. He gives his brother the motivation to keep going.

TRIUMPH The boys have competed in dozens of races. They have never finished first, but they always cross the finish line—together.

LOVING SUPPORT

We received a lot of attention after the boys were named *Sports Illustrated Kids* SportsKids of the Year in 2012. We met LeBron James at the awards ceremony, and he was so moved, he flew our entire family to Miami to watch him play.

MY LIFE The journey has been filled with plenty of ups and downs, but my boys—Cayden, Cooper and Conner—give me the reason to keep going every day.

Jeff was silent, wrestling with thoughts of his own. He had no answers for me.

"Why do we have to wait two days for an MRI?" I said. "I want to know right now."

He pulled into our driveway, and we sat in the car for a few seconds. Neither of us felt like moving. If the kids woke up and started crying, then we'd have to tend to them, so we just sat there, silent, absorbing the news and feeling the weight of it press down on us.

"I'm gonna call my dad," I said.

"No!" Jeff insisted.

"O.K., how about Ashley then? I have to talk to somebody," I said.

"No reason to get them all worried," Jeff said. "We handle our own business."

I knew Jeff cared deeply about Cayden, so deeply that he couldn't put those feelings into words. That was just his way, a way I had struggled to get used to because I am someone who likes to talk things through. I knew that Jeff's wall was up now, a wall of worry and fears. I also knew that at some point he'd say something, but right now it was too much for him to take on. So we didn't talk about it or share our worries, and I didn't call my dad.

For the next couple of days, life went on. Jeff went to work, and I took care of Conner and Cayden, all the while thinking through all the possible outcomes. If Cayden did have a tumor, we'd just have it removed and then we'd help him get better. I had been through that with my mother when she had cancer. It was painful, but at least I knew what that was like. And I had a lot of hope for Cayden's ability to put this behind him. He was so young, he'd have plenty of time to grow and recover from whatever was wrong. If it was something else, we'd deal with that problem the same way: figure it out and help Cayden get better. I reached the point where I was so focused on Cayden's recovery that it almost didn't matter what he had. I just wanted to know so we could start making him better.

A few days after the MRI, Jeff and I drove to hear Cayden's diagnosis from our new pediatric neurologist. The boys were with us, too. Whatever was wrong with Cayden, whatever needed to be fixed, was going to affect all of us.

The doctor's office wasn't like any other pediatrician's office I had ever been to. This was a dingy place with uncomfortable chairs and a rack of old magazines that had the covers half torn off. A nurse called our name and led us into the doctor's office. He was a somber man. He didn't smile or try to get to know us before he delivered the test results.

"Based on the tests, your son has ..."

He finished the sentence with words I didn't understand, something technical. I looked at Jeff and he looked back at me, confused.

"I'm sorry," I said. "We don't understand what you're saying."

"Your son has spastic cerebral palsy."

I had heard of cerebral palsy, but I wasn't sure what it was, so the doctor did his best to explain it to us simply.

"It's a muscle disorder," he said.

"How did he get such a thing? Is it genetic?" I asked.

"It comes from an injury to the motor centers of the brain. It could have happened before, during or shortly after birth," the doctor said.

"Was it that time when Cayden was having trouble breathing?

116

Right after he was born. Was that how he got cerebral palsy?" I asked.

"That's hard to know," he said. "Some brains just don't develop properly, and others sustain damage that stunts their development. What it means for the future is that your son will have a hard time controlling his muscles. That will be true for his entire life."

"His muscles. O.K., so you're telling me he'll have trouble moving his muscles. That's all it is? He is just going to move different?"

"Yes …" The doctor hesitated, trying to come up with another way to make all this information clear for us. "But there is a chance that he will never be able to walk. Many cerebral palsy patients have trouble communicating, too. His IQ will always be about half of what is normal for his age. He'll need help doing everything. Eating, bathing, everything."

"We can help Cayden with all that," I said quickly.

The doctor looked at me like I was naive and stupid and didn't understand reality.

"You'll probably need some time to consider your options," he said. "Taking care of Cayden will prove to be a big job. Probably a bigger job than you'll want to take on."

I looked at the doctor without saying a word. He must have thought I was confused again, because he continued.

"If you choose to take care of Cayden yourselves, he's going to rely on you for everything for the rest of his life. He'll never be able to live without you."

The doctor's tone was so negative. It was making me angry. I couldn't take it anymore, and I let my annoyance show.

"How can you be sure about what he'll be like when he's older?"

I asked. "Are you saying there's no hope? That he'll never be able to learn how to do anything on his own?"

"He might be able to learn a few things. You can try and try and try, but it won't stick."

"I can work with him," I told the doctor. "I can help him learn."

"You can try pushing him," the doctor replied. "But when a child has an IQ this low, your son won't be able to keep up. It's like trying to teach an old dog new tricks."

I couldn't accept what he was saying. I knew he had more experience and knowledge than we did, but he was making it sound like my family was doomed to fail. Then he struck his final blow.

"You should also know that about 80% of couples that take care of a child like Cayden end up getting a divorce. The pressure is just too much."

The conversation ended with the doctor setting up more appointments and tests to see if there was something wrong with Jeff and me genetically in case we wanted to have another child. As we gathered up the boys and started to make our way to the exit, the doctor did put his hand on Jeff's shoulder.

"I know it's a lot to take in, and that you want the best for your son," he said. "But really caring for a child with this handicap is a huge burden on a family. Please consider placing him in a home so you can pay attention to your other son. After all, you do have one healthy one there."

Jeff stiffened with anger. We walked out of the doctor's office in silence. I kept looking to him to say something, anything, about the enormity of the bad news we'd just received, but I could see from his set jaw that Jeff was furious.

As I strapped the boys in, Jeff got behind the wheel and just sat there for a minute stewing. I thought of that picture of the two brothers at the fishing hole, and tears welled up in my eyes. If this doctor was right, our boys would never be able to do those things together.

"Your son is going to be a burden on your family," Jeff said in a mocking voice that reflected his fury at the doctor. "You have one son who is O.K., but the other one is going to be a vegetable. He'll be in a wheelchair the rest of his life. He'll never leave your house. Put him in a home."

He dropped the phony voice and looked me directly in the eyes.

"We are a family," he said. "A family doesn't abandon one of their own."

"Not this family," I answered back.

Jeff and I had been raised in some pretty messed-up environments, and there were times when we ached for someone to show us attention and love, not just make sure that we were fed. We knew without discussing it that he and I wanted to hold ourselves to a higher standard as parents. We made Conner the center of our family, the focus of all of our attention and love even at those moments when Jeff and I had only harsh words for each other. We loved being a family, and now a doctor was taking a jackhammer to the foundation that we'd built in the years we'd been together.

Cayden may have had CP, but that didn't mean he didn't matter. He did matter. He mattered to us. We weren't going to send him away or settle for less than his fair share of everything in life: attention, opportunity and joy. As long as there was life in my body and strength in my heart, Cayden was not going to be cast aside. No. We were going to give him the best life he could possibly have, no matter what it cost us to make that promise come true. It wasn't just a fact for Jeff and me. That message got through to Conner as well. He was only 3 years old, but he was going to grow up knowing that his brother was not going to be left behind.

chapter sixteen

ACCEPTANCE

We never had a sit-down talk with Conner about his brother's condition. We never had to. He was with us when we learned that Cayden has CP, and he was with us as we all learned what that meant. Conner grew up seeing for himself what his brother does well and what he doesn't. He's never asked why Cayden can't walk or talk. He's never asked why Cayden has to sit in a special class in school or why he has CP. Really, he's only asked about two things when it comes to his brother: When can we find a sport to play together, and why do so many people stare at us when we go places?

The eyes that you feel when you're a special-needs family aren't always loving. They can be judging eyes, disapproving eyes. Conner can't express it that way just yet because he's still a boy, but I can. I have felt those eyes for most of my life. They're the eyes that people set on you when you're a high school dropout or the wife of a convict or a single mom. I have been all of those things, and I have felt the weight of those eyes.

On the rare occasion when we go out to a restaurant, all eyes are immediately on us. It's not surprising, because it's almost always a scene. It doesn't take much to set Cayden off. The lighting might be too bright for him, or not bright enough. CP makes him very sensitive to stimulation, and when it's too much he can react powerfully. Maybe the clinking and clattering of the dishes is too loud. It could be the music or the smells in the room. These are all triggers for Cayden, good mood or bad, and because of his CP he can't express how he feels the way most of us can. He can't calmly tell us what's making him excited or upset, and that's incredibly frustrating to him. So he expresses himself in the only ways he can control to get our attention. His voice gets loud. He squeals and whoops. He grunts. Of course, that makes people turn their heads.

When Cayden is upset, he starts banging his arms against his chair and swinging wildly in the air. He'll grab a tablecloth if he gets his hands on one. He'll knock over glasses or silverware. It's a parade of chaos, and it makes everyone tense.

Some people scowl at us in restaurants, annoyed that their quiet night is being disturbed. Others show pity, their eyes dropping in sadness as they try to ignore us. Some parents judge us for being unable to control our boy. Most people simply stare with curiosity. Children whisper to their mom or dad, pointing at us as they ask, "What's wrong with him?"

Everyone in my family has felt those eyes, every day. After a while, it wears on you because it feels like judgment. The judgment makes Jeff clam up. It makes me feel shame. For Conner, it just makes him want to defend and protect his brother.

"Why are those people looking at us so funny?" he used to ask me. Sometimes he'd go right up to a stranger staring at us and just start talking.

"Hi, my name is Conner. Let me introduce you to my brother, Cayden."

When I'd ask Conner why he did that, he'd simply shrug. "If they're staring," he'd say, "they must want to have a conversation."

JEFF AND I didn't put much thought into our decision to care for Cayden on our own. We acted out of emotion, not knowledge. I knew what it was like to see someone you loved only on weekend visits—I lived through it with BJ and even earlier when my mom was sick in the hospital. After his year in prison, Jeff also knew how hopeless it felt to be locked away. Neither of us could stand the thought of that happening to our innocent little boy.

But we also didn't know what would be demanded of us. I tried to fill that gap with a trip to the public library. Looking through the *C* volume of the encyclopedia, I saw pictures of kids with cerebral palsy that made me gasp. Their bodies looked so pained, with bones jutting in all directions, feet twisted at odd angles and knees that turned inward.

Was that what Cayden's limbs would do as he grew older? What effect would that have on his body? How long would he live? And most important to me, were there any treatments to make it better? The books didn't have those answers. They couldn't tell me what Cayden was going to be like tomorrow or the next day.

I started asking the doctors. I had many long conversations about treatments and cures. Some mentioned stem-cell research, others just flat-out told me that the only thing we could do was medicate Cayden to help him with his pain.

I felt a lot of anger in those early days after Cayden's diagnosis.

I was angry at the doctors for not having what I wanted—a treatment plan—and I was angry with myself for not being able to understand what I could do to help him. Sometimes I thought that maybe if I had stayed in school and gone to college I'd be smart enough to help Cayden. I needed explanations just to understand the explanations of my son's condition.

The one thing I never questioned was the decision that we would take care of Cayden ourselves. What could someone else do for our son that Jeff and I couldn't? The doctors were clear with us that because there was no miracle cure for CP, the only thing we could do was care for Cayden. Who would be better qualified to show him love and care than his family? Besides, this was our son—our responsibility—not a problem to be handed off to a nurse or an institution.

At first the job of caring for Cayden wasn't very different from caring for any baby. He needed to be fed and bathed and changed. He had medicines to take for the CP, and sometimes those medicines made him sick or sleepy, but in those early months caring for him wasn't that much different from what I had experienced with Conner.

The real difference was that Cayden didn't grow out of these phases. He never stopped needing diaper changes, even when his body grew to a size that made that whole process difficult. He never developed the ability to speak for himself, even though he developed preferences for what he wanted to eat or where he wanted to be. His inability to speak or focus his eyes also made me feel like I couldn't truly connect with our son.

In the early years, my growing realization that what the harsh doctor had said was right was very hard for me to accept.

Day after day I did my best to show Cayden love, but there were few ways to know if he felt that love coming through. He couldn't control his muscles, so he couldn't turn his head toward me and look me in the eyes. He wouldn't even let me hug him, his arms and legs flailing whenever I tried to embrace him. Many times I got poked in the eye trying to give my son a hug.

Cayden wasn't trying to hurt me—he just couldn't control his growing body. As his arms and legs became longer and more powerful, it became harder and harder to wrestle with him just to change a diaper or slip on a pair of pants. I'd be lying if I said it wasn't the hardest test of patience I've ever had to endure. You couldn't blame Cayden for the way he thrashed his body about—but it certainly wasn't convenient.

When Cayden was about 3, we had a breakthrough—a huge one. We bought him a wheelchair, and he learned to move around on his own power. Until then, Jeff or I had been carrying him wherever we went.

The first day in the chair, he just sat there, unable to find enough strength in his hands and arms to even try to inch forward. I honestly didn't know if he'd ever be able to move that chair by himself—after about 10 minutes of our rooting him on and showing him how it was done, he had given up even trying.

"He'll pick it up," the doctor told us. "He just needs time."

Sure enough, a week later, he was able to move himself and the chair—just a little bit, but it was a triumphant start. A few weeks after that, he could wheel across the room. Before we knew it, Cayden was throwing a fit if anyone tried to do the pushing for him. He couldn't talk, but his message was clear: My chair. I choose where to go.

The practical challenges of Cayden's condition were tough,

but they were nothing compared with the emotional hurdles I felt every day. I had so much love for Cayden, but it was hard for me to feel that love coming back in the ways I was used to. Imagine not being able to hold your child close. Imagine knowing that you'd never hear that voice say "I love you."

Late at night, when Cayden was asleep and his body was still and resting, I'd sneak into his bed and cuddle up beside him—just like I used to do with my mom—and pretend that he didn't have CP. I imagined having conversations with him. I imagined what he'd tell me, if he could just open his mouth and have the words come spilling out.

It was no different for Jeff, but the distance didn't seem to affect him as much, maybe because he was working all the time and maybe because he was a man with a different expectation for how to show affection.

Conner was quietly developing his own ways of bonding with his brother. They didn't play together like other siblings—no afternoons spent with Legos or other toys—but they developed a bond nonetheless because Conner was always mindful of his brother. He spoke to him directly. He asked him questions—what do you want to eat for dinner or watch on TV?—and he wasn't particularly bothered when there wasn't an answer coming back. In short, he respected his brother and treated him as an equal, not someone who was invisible. Cayden returned that affection simply by being comfortable around his Bubba.

As Cayden grew to toddler size, I made peace with the pattern of our lives. Each day could be filled with countless frustrations— messes, spills, tantrums—but there were also tiny moments of hope. You just had to train yourself to find those moments and appreciate them.

Other days were nothing but struggles, Cayden's development frozen in place and bad habits forming that I didn't know how to stop. When he was about $3^1/_2$, Cayden started to bite himself when he was upset. He would bite his arms, the only place he could easily reach, and he'd clinch his jaw down so hard that he drew blood. The doctor prescribed medicine to stop the habit, but all the medicine seemed to do was make Cayden tired all the time. This filled me with despair. I worried that he was miserable and frustrated, smarter than anyone gave him credit for being but unable to express all that was in him.

I figured Cayden was biting and screaming because he was trying to tell the world that he was here—he had something to give and share—but none of us could understand him because he couldn't speak. Since none of the doctors could help us find a way to give him a voice, they just gave him all that medicine to calm him down and numb his frustration.

With Conner in school and Cayden in a constant sleepy haze, there was no opportunity for the boys to bond together in obvious ways. No time to play. Conner never asked about the fishing trips we had always promised him with his brother, but I thought about them often. The doctors were right. Those moments were never going to happen, and the reality of that loss sent me into a gloom that bordered on depression.

Jeff never asked me what was wrong. He was like my half brother Tucker: Words failed him when he tried to express feelings, so he gave up on words and felt overmatched when I expressed mine. He coped with our situation by working longer hours and taking weekly fishing trips with Conner.

For me, the stress and gloom took its toll. I wasn't eating well or taking care of myself. I put on weight. I started to resent Jeff's stoic silence. I was careful about never giving the kids anything less than my best, but I'm sure I wasn't always a happy person to be around for them either, and I was definitely not the happiest when it was just Jeff and me alone in silence. There was so much I wanted to talk about, but that was not Jeff's way.

One day Conner asked me a simple question: "What's wrong, Mom?"

I wasn't sure how to answer. I didn't have all the answers for myself, let alone him. So I just told him nothing was wrong and I was just tired.

At moments like those, Conner always found a way to make me smile. He'd tell me a stupid joke or make noises like a duck. Small things, but thoughtful things to show me that he cared and wanted me to be happy.

I will always treasure those moments because those are the moments that kept me going. When I wasn't changing diapers and cleaning up, I was always plotting, searching for a way to make our life better and me a happier person for the rest of the family.

I started to obsess over ways I could make my life more positive. Maybe I could contribute to a support group to help other special-needs families. I had grown close online to so many other mothers like me. I leaned on those moms for support—they were the ones who encouraged me to tell the doctor that Cayden's sleepy haze was unacceptable and that he had to find another medicine to calm him down. That kind of help was invaluable to me, and I wanted to pay it forward and offer encouragement to other special-needs families if I could find a way.

One of my other obsessions became trying to teach Cayden sign language. Someone had shared an article with me that said some CP kids were able to learn sign, and I fell in love with the possibility that this might be a way for Cayden to express himself.

Day after day, week after week, I tried to teach Cayden one or two simple signs. He didn't really seem interested, and many signs were hard for him to form because he couldn't get his fingers and hands to make the finer movements.

I most wanted to teach Cayden the baby sign for "I love you." It seemed easy enough. You just hold up one hand with the pinkie, the pointer finger and the thumb all standing up and the middle two fingers held down against your palm. Then you gently twist your wrist. I showed Cayden that sign over and over, but it wasn't sticking. I held his fingers in place and told him what it meant.

"I love you! This means 'I love you.'"

I kissed his cheeks to show the meaning another way, without using words.

He smiled. He loved the attention. But he could never form the sign with his hand. That night when Jeff came home from work, he found me upset.

"What's wrong?" he asked.

There was really no way to fully answer that question for Jeff without it blowing up into a breakdown or a fight. I had told him many times before, "I need more of your help. I need more of your support." But nothing ever really changed. So I answered his question simply.

"I can't get Cayden to learn the sign for 'I love you.'"

Jeff seemed relieved.

"Let me work with him on it some," he said.

For the next several days, I saw Jeff sitting with Cayden in the mornings before he left for work. At first, he tried teaching

Cayden the sign I had failed with, the proper sign for "I love you."

"I don't know that his hand can make that sign," Jeff finally said.

That weekend Jeff had a fresh idea to help Cayden express himself.

"I've come up with a new sign for 'I love you,'" Jeff announced to me, Conner and Cayden over dinner.

He balled up his right hand into a fist and tapped it against his heart twice.

"From now on, that's our sign for 'I love you.' Hear that, Cayden? This means 'I love you.'"

He did it again. Conner watched Jeff and laughed. It reminded him of what they saw football players do when they watched games together on Sundays.

"Show your brother how to do it, Conner."

Conner followed right along, bumping his chest with his fist two times fast.

"Watch what Bubba does, Cayden!" he said. "I love you!"

Cayden was laughing now, too, watching his father and brother. Soon, I joined in.

"I love you! I love you!"

Cayden didn't make the new sign. But he watched. And he smiled.

A few days later, I awoke to find Cayden out of his bed. He wasn't anywhere in his bedroom, but there was a dirty diaper in there. Cayden had twisted and turned his way out of it during the night.

I sighed.

I walked into the living room to find Cayden alone, content, pulled up on the couch waiting for the world to join him. He was wearing his pajama top, and from the waist down he was completely naked.

I smiled a little and picked up my son.

"Good morning, Cayden. Let's get you cleaned up."

I brought Cayden to the bathroom and started running the water for a bath. Soon the tub was filled with warm water. I lowered Cayden into the tub, then started washing him up. When we were done with our unscheduled chore, I pulled Cayden out of the water. I never really joined Jeff and Conner on their "man time" fishing trips, but I imagined that this was my equivalent: wrestling a slippery whopper of a little boy out of the bathtub.

The job done, I started to help Cayden get dressed. He was happy, even playful with me. He didn't want to put on clothes, he wanted to stay wrapped in his soft snuggly towel.

"We have to get dressed, Cayden," I said quietly. "We have to get ready for the day."

I pulled a T-shirt over his arms one at a time, saving the hard part—his head—for last. Next came his pants. My, the boy had some long legs. I missed those snap-on pants from when he was a baby—it was so much easier.

It was still early in the morning—Conner and Jeff were asleep—but the unexpected detour of bathing Cayden, cleaning up his room and stripping his soiled sheets had already made me tired. When I was a teenager I would have just crawled back into bed and blown off whatever I was supposed to do next. But you can't blow off being a mother.

I sighed again and closed my eyes for a second, looking to find my second wind to make it through the rest of the morning.

When I opened my eyes I looked down to see Cayden. He was

smiling at me. Then he took his right hand and balled it into a fist, pounding his heart twice. I love you.

My heart soared. Why now? How did he know that was exactly what I needed? I bent down and kissed Cayden's head. Those were the special moments—the moments that kept me going.

chapter seventeen

LOVE

I know how much my boys love each other. I know it from the small kindnesses that they show every day.

With Conner, I see it in the way he speaks to his brother. His voice is always patient and kind. He includes his brother in his life when others choose to ignore him. He protects his brother from the nastiness of teasing and bullies. He stands up for Cayden even if he doesn't like the way a grownup treats his brother. It's never a scene or a confrontation, but he'll come to me and whisper in my ear when he thinks something is wrong.

With Cayden, it's there in the way he relaxes around Conner. He trusts his brother. He looks up to him. He admires him. Cayden is his best self whenever he's around Conner because he is at ease. He knows that someone is right nearby who understands him, respects him and cares for him. With other people, especially strangers, Cayden can be high-strung and on edge. With Conner, he is at peace.

Most days the feelings my boys share for each other aren't shown in grand gestures. They are measured in small moments: in cookies saved and jokes told, in mornings spent together over breakfast and trips to the YMCA basketball courts. It's in the way Cayden laughs when he rolls up and down the ramp at the park because he knows Conner is playing right nearby on the jungle gym. It's in the way Conner hugs his brother to say good night when it's time for bed, or when he walks across to Cayden's room to soothe him in the middle of the night because he hears his brother wake up upset—from a bad dream or because his stomach is aching from his medicine or because he's been fighting a cold and no one knows it yet because he can't tell us in words that he's feeling under the weather. Those are the moments that matter most in life. All the small kindnesses. Those are the moments that add up to love.

———————

I USED TO wonder how Conner learned how to be such a good brother. Both Jeff and I had brothers of our own, but we weren't really close to them. I pretty much saw my brother Tucker only at the holidays, even though he lived just half an hour away. The 16-year age difference was part of it. We had never lived in the same house when I was young, and it was difficult to stay in touch with him when I moved in with my father after my mother died.

Tucker was never fully able to deal with the loss of my mom. He handled emotions the same way Jeff did. When he felt things deeply, he didn't like to talk about them. Tucker also suffered from depression. Although his condition was never diagnosed by a doctor, I'm pretty sure it was true because my brother would spend weeks feeling so down that he was unable to leave his house or answer the phone. I tried to help, but even when I took the time to drive to his house and sit with him face to face, Tucker was hard to reach. He could be so distant and so sad. Knowing my brother was unhappy in life didn't lessen my shock the day I received that call from the police. Tucker had taken his life, shooting himself while sitting on the couch in his home. He was alone.

I learned more about my brother in death than I ever knew from talking to him. His friends told me how he wanted to take me in after our mom died, but he knew he wouldn't be able to take care of both of us. They also told me that he was always worried about me during my years with BJ, tempted many times to drive over to try to protect me and save me from my own mistakes. But like so many people in my life, Tucker didn't have the strength to match his good intentions.

In death, Tucker did leave me with a precious gift: his house and the land it sat on in Hendersonville, Tennessee. The property had belonged to his father's parents, and they left it to him when they passed. It was a beautiful piece of land. Tucker built a cabin there himself, perched up on a hill overlooking a field and a big, glistening pond. When the lawyers told me and Jeff that Tucker had left his land and home to me, we were overwhelmed.

We knew the farm would be a great place to raise the boys, even though I was haunted by the fact that my brother had taken his life in that house. There was still a hole in the window in the living room, a mark left by the bullet Tucker used. We hung burgundy curtains to cover it, but I always knew. Whenever I looked out that window, I thought about Tucker and his sadness.

The day we moved in, the eighth move I had made since I was 12 years old, the boys were in the backseat, Conner staring out the window at the fields and farms passing by. Cayden was looking out the window too, drifting in and out of sleep. I held the snow globe my mother had given me safely in my lap. I couldn't let that break. I thought a lot about family as we drove down the long, isolated roads. Pretty much everything I cared about was in that car with me. This was my life. Precious as the snow globe, and just as fragile.

As I looked back in the rearview mirror to check on the boys, I noticed Cayden's head was at a crooked angle while he slept. It looked uncomfortable, like it was going to hurt his neck. Conner must have been thinking the same thing, because without my saying a word, he leaned over and lifted his brother's head until it came to rest against the back of his car seat.

We weren't perfect parents. And heaven knows we weren't perfect people. But somehow our boys knew a lot about love, and that made me proud.

Maybe it was living on that great big farm, but Jeff and I started talking more seriously than ever about getting married. We had our stresses and fights, but we were five years into our life together. Our personalities couldn't be more different—mine outgoing and loud, and his so quiet and reserved—but I truly appreciated Jeff. I loved him. He never formally proposed, and neither did I, but we both agreed that it was time to become a family legally as well as being a family of the heart.

We decided that the best place to exchange vows was on the farm. We could have as many people as we pleased there, and the setting would be beautiful. The ceremony was held outside in the field that overlooked the pond. I wore a white wedding dress with silver embellishments, a real wedding dress, not like the one I picked out from the maternity store when I married BJ in prison. My father marched me proudly across the field to meet Jeff and the pastor. He was dressed in his suit, his hair neatly trimmed and combed. This was like his finish line, a milestone that showed he had done his best to help raise his daughter to a fully grown adult. My ring was fashioned from a gold necklace that my grandmother had given me, one with a tiny diamond pendant. I loved that ring. It was not big or showy. It was a piece of love passed down from my grandmother to me, and now it was a symbol of the new family Jeff and I had created together.

As Jeff and I spoke our vows, I felt proud of how far both of us had come in life. I didn't know what the future was going to hold for us, but I had hope. My life had been full of confusion and chaos, but love had brought me forward to this beautiful day. As I watched Conner dance the Worm at our reception and share giggles with Cayden, I couldn't imagine life being much better. It was one of the happiest days of my life.

In the year that followed our wedding, Jeff and I settled into a steady and predictable life. He worked and fished. I looked after the boys. It wasn't glamorous, but it was dependable. Whenever I felt down, all I had to do was look at my boys and it kept me going. They were my reward and my hope for the future.

Eventually, Jeff and I decided to sell Tucker's house and land in Hendersonville—it proved to be too sad a reminder of Tucker and his troubles. We used the money to buy a small ranch home of our own in White House, Tennessee, a suburb about a half hour from downtown Nashville. The house was on a quiet cul-de-sac, a safer place for the kids to play. It also had the side benefit of reminding me of my childhood in Old Hickory. I imagined Conner riding around that neighborhood on his bike with his friends, roaming from house to house, just as I had done when

I was a child. The other advantage of the new house was that its three bedrooms and two baths were all on one floor. That made it easier for Cayden to get around in his wheelchair. He was getting to be a big boy. He was always slim, but heavy if you had to carry him up and down a flight of stairs. In our new home that wouldn't be a problem.

This was the very first place either Jeff or I had ever owned on our own. Who would believe it? For a while I didn't. I felt as if this were some kind of a dream: me and my family in a home of our own after all the screwups and mistakes. Who would have thought? It reinforced my belief in the power of second chances.

On November 25, 2009, I gave birth to our third son, a healthy little boy we named Cooper. Right from the start, Cooper was a spitfire: a blond pixie full of energy and mischief. Conner and Cayden already had their bond, but they quickly accepted Cooper as their pesky—and loved—little brother. A third child seems to grow up while you're not even looking, and before we knew it Cooper was a toddler who loved annoying his brothers by hanging around Conner's room uninvited or pushing Cayden for unwanted joyrides in his wheelchair.

Jeff was doing well as an electrician. Now that we were so close to Nashville, he was able to take on jobs wiring hotels and office buildings. We weren't rich—or even comfortable—but the days of being able to afford to eat only a couple packs of ramen noodles every night were thankfully behind us.

For me, looking after the three boys was a full-time job—and a hard one. Just as that doctor told us, Cayden relied on me for everything from the time he woke up until the time Jeff came home from work at night to help me out. I fed Cayden. I changed his diapers. I bathed him. I played with him. And I loved him.

The one thing the doctor was absolutely wrong about was that Cayden would never be able to learn things. They never found any underlying medical issues with Cayden beyond the CP, and I know he tries very hard to retain the things he learns at school or that I teach him. At school, Cayden has an Individualized Education Program, or IEP, where his teachers and I set goals for him each semester. The goals are simple compared with those for other children his age—like learning to recognize shapes and colors. And Cayden doesn't learn as fast or as well as most of the other kids, but he does learn. He meets his goals for school every year. If you sit down to teach Cayden, everything has to be done visually because he can't communicate vocally. But if you put out boards with numbers and ask him to point to a 7, he can do it without much trouble.

It still makes me angry to think back to that doctor who warned us that he would never be able to learn. They made us believe that our son might not even have a working brain in his head. But he can point to the foods he wants to eat, he can laugh at jokes, he can play with toy cars—he even hangs his head when I have to scold him for misbehaving. Cayden can learn, and I won't ever give up on that.

Sometimes, when I see Cayden with other children or adults who don't have the time—or desire—to tune in to his frequency, I get frustrated. They just choose to ignore him, act like he's not really there. He is there, and I'm positive he knows a lot about what's going on around him.

If anything, the older Cayden has gotten, the more aware we are of how capable and loving he is. He is an amazing child, considering everything he has to endure. He laughs and smiles in a way I wish I could, his eyes full of carefree happiness.

One of Cayden's greatest pleasures is taking a bath. He loves the feeling of the warm water and of my hands gently shampooing his hair. It's so peaceful for him, and he can't get enough of the bliss. Watching him enjoy the water, I wish I could lose myself in such simple pleasures. But usually my mind is too filled and distracted—by my chores, by my to-do list, by my worries.

Cayden doesn't lament the things he is missing. He simply loves the life he has. That makes me want to keep going for him because I can give him a home, I can give him safety, and I can surely give him love and attention.

Everyone in our family feels that way about Cayden, perhaps Conner most keenly of all. Jeff and I said right after the diagnosis that we were going to do everything we could to give Cayden the best life possible. What we didn't realize was that Conner was going to play a huge role in not only giving Cayden a better life than any of us could have imagined—he was also going to change the lives of all of us in the process.

Everything that had happened to us—the good and the bad—was all about to come full circle and miraculously send us off in a new, positive direction. And it would all start with that promise we made to Conner before Cayden was even born—a promise that he never let go of. It was the promise that one day, he and his brother were going to play sports together. After Cayden was born, we were convinced that promise wasn't even possible. And we never could have imagined where it would lead.

— chapter eighteen —

REWARD

Conner and Cayden had never played a sport together—never felt the thrill of a race or the powerful bond of teamwork when individuals come together to achieve a goal. They had played together outside, Conner running around the playground and Cayden wheeling around nearby. They had bonded as brothers by spending time together indoors over meals and in front of the TV. But never any sports.

That bothered Conner. He loved sports, the rush when your heart starts pumping and your body loosens up. Competition and challenge, will and focus, reaching, striving, pushing, trying and ultimately achieving ... It all happens in sports. Conner so wanted to share that feeling with his brother. He asked about it all the time.

Basketball, football, fishing ... Conner wanted his brother to be right there with him. Jeff and I tried. We always brought Cayden along, but it was never enough to satisfy Conner. He wanted more.

"I want to play sports WITH Cayden," he'd say. "I want him to feel what it's like to play, too. That's the fun! It's not the same off to the side."

Cayden must have felt the same way, because he grew antsy fast whenever he was stuck on the sidelines in his wheelchair. He'd look up to the sky and grunt, spinning in circles to get our attention. "I'm BORED" is what he'd be telling us. "I don't want to be HERE."

As a parent, you always try to give your children what they want if you can. But this was something we couldn't give the boys. We couldn't give Cayden a body that would let him play sports the same way Conner could. And we couldn't give Conner the chance to share sports with Cayden the way that he wanted.

So there it was. Reality. We couldn't do it. We're talking about sports here, but it applies to other things in life, too. We couldn't do it. But Conner and Cayden could. They figured out a way to truly play together because they never stopped trying.

———————

IT WAS JUST an ordinary spring afternoon. Conner was home from school, and he and I were sitting on the couch together while Cayden played with Matchbox cars and Cooper napped. I was flipping through a parenting magazine when I saw a picture from the Nashville Kids Triathlon in an ad that encouraged people to sign up. If Conner hadn't been next to me, I would have flipped right past that page.

"What's that?" Conner asked, placing his finger on the ad.

"It's a race for kids," I said.

"What kind of race?"

"A triathlon. That's a race with biking, swimming and running. It looks like they're having one for kids."

"That would be fun," Conner said. "Maybe we can do that race. Can we sign up?"

"You really want to?" I asked, thinking about the entry fee that wasn't in our budget and the equipment he'd need to compete. Conner had a bike, but not a very good one.

"Yeah. I want to. I want to do it with Cayden, too."

I shook my head in frustration. We had had conversations like this before. I thought it would be like basketball and football all over again.

"We can put a trailer on my bike," Conner continued. "I've seen those. And I can push him in that trailer, too, while I run."

I was listening. I could picture it.

"You know you have to swim too …" I said.

"Dad could tie a rope around me and I could pull Cayden behind me on a raft!"

I sat for a moment thinking about this crazy idea. Conner wanted to pull, push and drag Cayden all around Centennial Park. To hear Conner talk, it all sounded possible.

The race required kids in Conner's age group to swim 100 yards, cycle three miles and run a half-mile, all three stages back to back to back.

Later that afternoon, I described the race to Cayden. I told him about Conner's plan, too.

"Do you want to do that with your Bubba? Does that sound like fun?"

Cayden immediately broke out into a huge grin and started clapping his hands together. He was in. As far as the boys were concerned, the race was set. They were going to enter.

Now all Jeff and I had to figure out was how to make it work.

I called the race organizers to ask if they would let my sons, ages 7 and 5, compete as a team, a very unusual team. I had a flutter of fear that the officials wouldn't allow them to compete, but the opposite was true. They got so excited about what the boys were trying to do, they waived the entry fee. I should have taken this as a sign of all the good things to come when we opened up our lives to this adventure, but instead all I could think about was my next worry: gear.

Conner's bike was an orange and gold Huffy that cost about $99 at Walmart. Where was I going to find a trailer to fit on that? I told a friend about our crazy plan, and she offered us her brother's trailer, which he and his family hadn't used in a while. We grabbed it.

With the boys officially signed up for the race, the next step was practice. The race was only a few days away when we placed Cayden, barefooted, in the trailer Jeff had just attached to the Huffy. It was all new to Cayden, and at first he wasn't so sure about getting in that trailer. When he's unsure, he'll let you know with whoops and flailing arms. But once Cayden was strapped in, he started to calm down. This was different: We were all together, outside, and he seemed to know something was about to happen. Something fun.

We gave Conner the O.K., and he took off down the cul-de-sac. Conner pedaled as fast as he could to the end of the block, standing up on his pedals to give them a little extra speed, and turned around to race back to where Jeff and I stood. I could hear Cayden laughing all the way down the street. He loved the rush of speed and the feeling of the wind against his skin as Conner pushed that Huffy as fast as his legs could carry them.

Just the sight of it made my heart swell. Conner was giving his brother pure joy.

Even if the boys never made it to the race, this was something we had never experienced before. The boys were bicycling together and loving it. Seeing that, I started to believe that this really was going to work. Our boys were going to race together. Now I was excited.

Sure, our way of competing was haphazard. Some parents might have told Conner that he would have to practice on his own, and also spend time with Cayden at his side, before he could even consider entering a race with kids who likely had been training and competing for years. For our boys, we just signed them up and pulled everything together in a few days. We knew they'd never finish first. In fact, they'd likely finish last—if they were able to finish at all. But the point was to have fun and try to make it to the end, not to get the first-place medal. The race itself was going to be the reward. My boys would be swimming and biking and running alongside kids their age for the first time ever, and for us, that was enough.

Word of the boys' entry into the race spread quickly through the congregation at the church we attended in White House, a nondenominational Christian church called Revolution. Suddenly we had people eager to come and cheer on the boys. I decided to get neon green T-shirts printed with TEAM LONG BROTHERS on them so that the boys would be able to pick our cheering section out of the crowd. I was so touched that our little world was rallying around Conner and Cayden.

The day before the race, all the participants were required to report to Centennial Park in downtown Nashville, where we would meet a woman named Mandy Gildersleeve. Mandy was the racecourse coordinator who agreed to shadow the boys to make sure everything went smoothly and to rescue them if there was any trouble. Mandy was perfectly suited to the task of keeping track of a differently abled competitor. She had raced before with a young boy who was an amputee.

We saw Mandy standing by a big tent filled with racers and their families. She looked fit and strong, with short dark hair and a welcoming smile that eased my anxiety. Her voice was warm and friendly. Cayden gave her his stamp of approval by not freaking out.

"I've raced with special-needs kids before," she reminded us. "But I've never seen two brothers competing in a race as a team. This is going to be so cool."

I loved her attitude! She didn't scowl as if she thought they would never finish. She was as inspired by this as our friends from church and the race organizers. Suddenly I felt we had momentum, as if for the first time in our lives, the whole world was pulling for our little family, and all because of Conner's crazy idea.

As Mandy showed us the main hub of the racecourse, an area they called Transition, she explained to Conner how everything was going to work the next day.

"You're going to start the race with the swim," she said to Conner. "When you swim, you're going to weave like a snake, down the first lane then up the next, down the third, then back up the fourth. That's 100 yards."

Conner listened calmly.

"When you're done with the swim, we'll have your bike waiting. After we strap in Cayden, I'll be riding along with you to help if anything goes wrong. The cycling path winds through the park, and there are a couple of hills, but nothing you can't handle," Mandy said with a smile. "You'll be fine. When you finish cycling, you'll leave your bike and start the run. The running trail is across the park, and back again. That's it. Then you cross the finish line with Cayden!"

She made it all sound so simple! And I guess it was, if you were an experienced athlete. When I thought of dragging Cayden for almost four miles, I felt exhausted in advance. Conner had never done any kind of race like this before, and as far as swimming, well, the only stroke he knew was the dog paddle.

When we got home, I made myself busy laying out clothes and snacks for the next morning. I wanted everything in order and ready to go, because we had to be at Centennial Park at 6:30.

Jeff channeled his nerves into checking and rechecking all the equipment. Out in the garage, he filled the bike tires with air and blew up our orange raft. We looked more ready for a day at the lake than for a triathlon, but ready or not, this was about as prepared as we were going to be.

The alarm buzzed the next morning just before 5, and the day greeted us with total darkness. For breakfast, I wanted there to be healthy stuff for the boys, so I put out granola bars and bananas. Cayden, of course, wanted his Froot Loops. He got what he wanted.

Jeff rechecked the car to make sure we had all the equipment. Then we were off.

The sun was shining bright by the time we reached the city. We must have been a sight as we made our way through the park. Jeff and me in our neon green TEAM LONG BROTHERS T-shirts; Conner in his $6 red and black swim trunks with skeletons printed on them and a brand-new pair of blue running shoes;

and Cayden in his wheelchair, wearing a SpongeBob helmet.

Jeff was sweating and silent, which meant he was nervous. The anxiety of the race and the crowd surrounding us were exactly the type of things Jeff tried to avoid, and noise and commotion like that wasn't always the best atmosphere for Cayden, either. Yet we made it through without any upsets. While I pushed Cayden through the crowd in his wheelchair, Conner pulled the empty jogging stroller that was attached to his bike and Jeff walked behind him, inspecting all the equipment over and over again with his eyes.

The sun beat down on our heads like a spotlight. You could feel the energy of the moment all bubbling at the bottom of your stomach waiting to be released. Is this what pro athletes feel like on game day? It had to be.

Then it happened.

POW!

Jeff and I spun around. Other people turned to look, too. It sounded like a blast from a gun. One of the two tires holding up the back of the trailer had burst wide open. We weren't bike people. We didn't have a spare tire. We had no idea what to do. The first thought that flashed into my mind was "There goes the race."

The disappointment must have shown on my face, because Conner looked at me with an expression that said, "Please don't tell me we can't do this."

Before I could say a word, Jeff was gone. There just wasn't enough time for him to make it to a store and back before the race, but he took off anyway. The boys and I had nothing to do but keep walking toward the starting line. I needed to find Mandy.

Finally, standing near a tent surrounded by the dogwoods and magnolias of the park, I saw that smile.

I showed Mandy the busted tire.

"Don't worry about it," Mandy said. "Conner doesn't need that tire inflated. He can just race with it the way it is. We'll make it work."

Race with it the way it is, and make it work. Perfect. That was our family motto.

I called Jeff on his cell phone. "Mandy says don't worry about the tire. Come back."

"What?"

"Yeah, just come back."

Before long, Jeff was right by my side for the national anthem to officially start the race. As we entered the park's Sportsplex, I saw our green-shirted boosters stomping and yelling their heads off. Jeff and I helped Cayden slip into his life jacket by the side of the pool. Looking around at this strange, huge building with red, white and blue flags and the shimmering floor of water, Cayden started to giggle. It was just like bath time to him, bath time in the biggest tub he'd ever seen. Cayden was excited.

Conner, determined, stepped into the pool as we helped Cayden, his life jacket already around his torso, into the raft. Then the horn sounded. Conner pulled his goggles over his eyes and dog-paddled down the first lane, pushing water with one hand and pulling the raft with the other. Kids passed Conner and Cayden as if they were standing still. Conner was smiling and oblivious to the kids who were passing them. I saw him look back at Cayden several times and take energy from that huge smile of his brother's. At the end of each lane, Conner stopped to lift his head and catch his breath.

"Woohoo! Go, Conner! Go, Cayden!" Our church cheering section kept the volume loud and constant. I wondered if Conner and Cayden could hear them over all the commotion.

Conner was pouring it all out in the pool. He was going full tilt, even if he wasn't going very fast. As he turned the final corner toward the finish of the swimming portion, around me our church group was making the loudest cheer I'd ever heard, all for my two boys.

As Conner paddled up to the ladder at the edge of the pool, Jeff snagged the raft and lifted Cayden out. Then we all started toward Transition, where the bike and trailer were waiting. We moved with urgency, but we were being careful with Cayden. For us, the clock didn't matter.

Our bike and trailer stood out amid the sleek new equipment most of the racers used. Ours was lopsided and low, but ready to go. As Mandy and Jeff situated the boys in their cockeyed chariot, my heart was high in my chest. They'd done what I considered to be the toughest part, and Conner's energy was still strong. He sped off down the path with all of his other competitors far ahead in the distance. From where I stood on the sidelines, all I saw was the back of the little blue lopsided trailer getting smaller and smaller. Oh God, I didn't like not being able to see them.

Three miles. How long would it take the boys to cover three miles?

Jeff came to my side, and we hugged without speaking a word. Then we just stood and looked at each other. Finally, Jeff broke the silence.

"I'm nervous," he said. "I'm going to walk up and see if I can get a better view."

"O.K. I'm staying here because I don't want to miss seeing them at the finish."

Almost 24 minutes passed. Mandy later told me that Conner was talking to his brother throughout the bike ride. "Are you O.K., Cayden? We're doing a great job. We're halfway there."

For parts of the bike ride, Mandy saw that Cayden had closed his eyes. The bliss on his face was the feeling of the breeze brushing across his cheeks. Mandy thought he might be sleeping, and it's possible that he nodded off a bit now and then. But I think he was just at peace. Whenever Conner spoke, his eyes would open and his head would lift to hear the message.

All along the trail, people stopped to cheer. "Way to go, boys! Keep on going!" Race volunteers. Police officers. Even dozens of basset hounds that were gathered near the bike path for an event in Centennial Dog Park—they barked with approval.

Finally, I could see them. First, Conner's blue helmet. Then the metal handlebars of that little orange bike. Then there was Cayden, grinning from ear to ear. Other kids were zooming past on their aerodynamic bikes, but there was the Huffy, chugging along like Santa's sleigh. I could see Mandy, and she was sweating. I knew that if she was sweating, Conner must be exhausted.

Then I saw Jeff and some of our friends from church. Jeff had tears in his eyes. You could tell how proud he was seeing his boys accomplish this together. Our friends were all snapping pictures and cheering. "You got this, boys! You got this."

Jeff slipped into Transition to unhook the trailer from the bike and attach the third wheel for the run. I came with him to give Conner some quick words of encouragement.

"You're doing great. You're doing amazing."

He was breathing heavily, but he was happy.

"It's hard out there," he said between gulps of air.

Now the boys were off again. Conner looked so small, pushing a jogging stroller built for an adult. The push bar was almost at the level of his eyes. Our friends started to scatter, looking for the best position to watch the final leg of the race. I stayed right by the finish line. I really wanted to be at the finish.

As I stood waiting for Conner and Cayden to appear through the trees lining 25th Avenue and cross the finish line, tears streamed down my cheeks. This wait felt almost as long as the bike ride, but I knew it was the last leg, and I allowed myself to anticipate the ending, the triumph of seeing them complete the race.

The eyes that I saw staring at me and the boys now were different. There wasn't judgment in these eyes. There was love, admiration and inspiration.

How strange everything seemed.

Maybe the bad looks I was feeling at all those low points in my life were really a reflection of how I was seeing myself: high school dropout, felon's wife, teen mom. That was my baggage, my shame, and it was probably time to drop the heavy load and do as Conner and Cayden were doing—just keep moving forward, just keep racing.

The clock officially timed the boys' run at 7 minutes, 27 seconds. But the joy I felt as I saw them take those final steps released a lifetime of emotions.

Cayden was clapping. Conner was screaming, and his hair was drenched with sweat. As Jeff reached down to lift Cayden out of the stroller, Cayden looked directly at his older brother and Conner beamed back. Cayden shifted his hand back to the front of his body and made a clumsy fist. He pounded his chest twice to let his brother know how grateful he was.

"I love you too, Cayden," Conner said.

All around us was chaos as camera crews filmed the boys making their way to get medals for completing the race. The race organizers placed medals around both boys' necks. Cayden was excited to play with his medal. This was his.

One of our friends from church picked Conner up and sat him on his shoulders. Now Cayden was getting irritated because the race had stopped. He didn't want it to end. If it were up to Cayden, he would have been pushed around the park 500 more times. We brought the boys to a little area away from the chaos of the finish line to try to calm down and relax. I handed the boys juice boxes. Here we were. We weren't supposed to be here, but we were.

Here at the race, people could see Cayden as he truly was—a wonderful, joyful little boy radiating positive light. I knew it. I felt it. People also saw Conner differently. He wasn't just a caring kid. He was an inspiration. People came up to Jeff and me, too. "You are such terrific parents," they said. "To raise boys who would do something like this …"

The truth is, nothing had changed between who we were before the race and who we were after. We were the exact same family that could cause a scene in a restaurant. We were the same imperfect people who had seen the walls of a prison. But outside, at a race in the park, we were the family everyone was cheering for. It truly was a miracle.

EPILOGUE

Since that day in Centennial Park, the boys have been in so many races I've lost count. They've run in 5K's and 10K's all over the South, in triathlons as far east as Pennsylvania and twice in the sport's biggest race: the IronKids Triathlon. When we went to Brock's Gap Intermediate in Alabama for a 5K, the whole school fell in love with the boys. We've gone back there three times and are planning to go this year as well.

Life changed in other ways, too, all because of racing. People grabbed onto Conner and Cayden and held them close to their hearts. It was astonishing to us. We went from being a family bumbling along to becoming a symbol of hope, of love's enduring bond and of countless other noble things that people projected onto us. We were on the go all the time, collecting awards from local and national organizations that focused on families with special-needs kids. We felt so grateful to receive the honors, and humbled. We knew full well that we were receiving those awards on behalf of countless families like ours—families that work hard to make sure the world doesn't ignore these precious, remarkable children who have so much to share if you just make the effort to recognize it.

Everything happened fast. We had overcome many dramatic and unexpected shifts in our life before, but this was the first time we ever had to deal with changes that were so *positive*. I can admit now that the first time I had a television camera stuck in my face, I panicked. We were suddenly surrounded by a more privileged set than anyone we'd rubbed shoulders with at the Piggly Wiggly. Everyone loved the great moment of watching my boys find their way to the finish line despite the challenges of Cayden's condition. But for a long while uneasiness still gnawed at me: What if these good people found out about the ragged path that our family had stumbled along before we even made it to that first race?

Then it hit me. This good feeling wasn't about me or Jeff, so none of our baggage should get in the way. The good feeling was a response to the true hearts of Conner and Cayden. My boys brought to life that framed picture I displayed in the nursery before Cayden was born: the image of two boys side by side at the fishing hole. As that picture was for me, the boys had become a symbol of love for everyone they encountered. Don't get me wrong about Conner and Cayden. They aren't saints. They are brothers, and they are human—prone to occasional spats and annoyances just like everyone else. But love *is* always shared between them. It holds them tightly together no matter what life throws their way. Conner couldn't take Cayden to the fishing hole, but he could give him something much more powerful: freedom and joy. What a gift.

That's the reason the cameras kept following us after the boys started racing. Newspapers, magazines, local TV crews. Even a documentary-film crew from Japan got wind of the boys' story. Ultimately it led to the whole family flying to New York City to appear on *Good Morning America*. It was quite a production getting a toddler, a wheelchair-bound child with special needs and a preadolescent from Tennessee to Times Square for the first time. But the experience was worth it.

We were sitting on a sofa on live television with Josh Elliott from *Good Morning America*. I was holding Cayden in my lap, which seemed to be calming him down despite all the lights and television cameras that moved around us, silent and invisible to anyone watching at home. Cayden's hands were waving around, but not too wide, as Conner described what racing with his brother meant to him. Then, suddenly, Bob Der, the editor of *Sports Illustrated Kids* and my co-author for this book, walked onto the set and announced that the boys had been named SportsKids of the Year. Another enormous honor!

It was all a shock, the thrill lingering in the air after the TV appearance was over, and Bob asked us to come with him to the *Sports Illustrated* offices so we could meet the staff. I'll never forget the walk from the ABC studio in Times Square to the Time & Life Building. Eight amazing blocks! So many people packed in tight—tourists, New Yorkers with their heads down racing to work, even people dressed like cartoon characters handing you things and trying to talk you into taking a picture with them. The lights from the shops and billboards teased your eyes to look up while the smell of street-food hot dogs practically grabbed you by the nose to tug you in a different direction altogether. It was hard to stay focused as an adult, so I can't even imagine what it was like for the boys.

We had to watch Cooper, our youngest, extra carefully because he seemed ready to run off to who knows where if we didn't clamp on to his hand tightly enough. Cayden always pitched a fit if anyone tried to steer his wheelchair, so we had to let him navigate the streets himself while we kept a watchful eye on him. He was meandering around, sometimes bumping into the people and things that were in his way—and every block offered a new set of obstacles and curiosities. Thankfully, we didn't have to worry about Conner. He stuck by our side, in full control of the situation, helping to look out for his brothers.

I looked over at Bob, a New Yorker who makes this walk every day but at that New York pace. It takes him only about 10 minutes to travel this distance alone, but as a group we slowed it down to about half an hour. Bob told me later that he feared we'd never make it. He experienced firsthand what it's like to get the boys from point A to point B. It's a process, and a stressful one if you aren't used to it.

That night, after Jeff and I got the whole circus back to the hotel room and wrangled the kids into bed, we sat there for a while, so exhausted, so overstimulated. We didn't have anything to say to each other—we were just overwhelmed. I knew Jeff was uncomfortable with what was happening, all the lights and cameras and staring eyes. The whole experience was exciting to me, but not because of the attention—I couldn't have cared less about that. I was excited about all the opportunities that the boys were unlocking. It wasn't just the opportunity for my sons to feel pride and fulfillment for what they had accomplished together; it was also the opportunity to help other families with special-needs children feel respect and love, too.

When we returned to New York a few weeks later to attend the official *Sports Illustrated* Sportsman of the Year ceremony, Jeff was not happy, and we weren't getting along. Jeff is a man of few words whose emotions run deep. He doesn't like social scenes, doesn't feel comfortable shaking hands and navigating rooms full of strangers—and that was happening all the time now. Jeff didn't want me to have to make a trip like this alone, but he didn't feel great being there, either. He would have rather been at work. And he would have *much* rather been at a fishing hole, alone, finding his peace with a rod and reel.

The *SI* Sportsman of the Year ceremony was a big, fancy party held in a big glass building in downtown Manhattan. Everyone watched us walk in down a long red carpet with flashbulbs exploding in our eyes. Even people passing on the street could look in to see all the fuss through the glass walls. That's the point of the event—it's a celebration, a victory lap meant to be seen.

Of course, all that attention made Jeff miserable. If it weren't for the responsibility of helping tend to the boys, I don't know if I could have kept him in that building for more than a minute. I felt bad that Jeff was so uncomfortable, but moments like that always reminded me how different we were as people. I am naturally outgoing and curious. Jeff is a loner who prefers his world to be smaller and more predictable.

The main attraction of the ceremony was basketball superstar LeBron James, *SI*'s choice for Sportsman of the Year. But before they got to honoring LeBron, they started the ceremony by celebrating the boys, the SportsKids of the Year.

The room was filled with hundreds of people—all in dresses and suits and ties. In the front rows alone you could see Jay Z and Beyoncé, Duke basketball coach Mike Krzyzewski and, of course, LeBron James. At first, no one knew who we were or why we were there. Then, after a brief introduction from Bob, the lights dimmed and a video started playing that told the story of the boys and their racing. The video footage showed Conner riding his bike and pulling Cayden along in the trailer as the sun was setting, but the voice you heard was Jeff's. He was remembering that day in the doctor's office when we first heard the harsh news about Cayden and his CP. In the video, Jeff was angry all over again—you could hear it in his voice—hurt by the indifference of the world as he recalled that doctor telling us to put Cayden in a home. "That doctor pretty much told us, you know, your son is going to be a burden on your family … You've already got one kid. He's O.K. This one has cerebral palsy. He's gonna be a vegetable. He'll be in a wheelchair the rest of his life. He'll never leave your house. Put him in a home." The way Jeff spit out those words, I remembered how he bristled with pride and fury the day of Cayden's diagnosis, and I remembered the instant strength of conviction that we both shared to take care of Cayden ourselves. It was our finest moment as a couple—a choice that helped lead to all that was happening now. After the video and the strong reaction it got from the audience—a standing ovation!—Jeff surprised us by joining me and the boys up on the stage—an act of pure love for the boys because I know how much it bothered him to be in front of all those staring eyes.

When LeBron James got up to accept his Sportsman of the Year award, he first wanted to talk about the boys. He looked right at Conner and said, "I don't have to preach anymore. I can just show my older son what he can do for his younger brother." When the ceremony was over, a long line of people rushed to us, eager to get close to the boys. In that line waiting to pay their respects were Jay Z and Beyoncé. Can you believe it? They were waiting to pay respect to us.

It was a great moment for our family. Unforgettable. But it was also tinged with sadness for me because in my heart I knew that Jeff and I were coming to a crossroads as a married couple. We were fighting more than usual—fighting about trivial nothings on the surface, but beneath all that we were fighting because we were such different people. Jeff, quiet but deeply feeling. Me, chatty and in need of talking through my worries and problems for fear that I might burst if I don't.

We tried a number of things to save our marriage, including counseling, but it was becoming clear that the stresses and strains were getting to be too much. About the only bond we shared deeply anymore was our love and commitment to the boys. When that started to feel compromised, too—children shouldn't have to watch their parents fight with each other all the time, and if the only resolution to those fights was silent brooding, what kind of lesson is that?—I knew we had reached a really unhealthy place as a couple.

Sadly, Jeff and I divorced in 2014. Jeff is still very involved with raising the boys. We split time with them equally, and I still think he's the most wonderful father I could ever wish for. I have a lot of regrets about the end of my marriage to Jeff. But one of the biggest is the impact it had on the boys. With all that going on, they could only compete in fewer than half the races they normally would. We've pledged to correct that in the upcoming season. Racing is their time together. It's their bond.

Even with our marital troubles, the world continued to reach out to the boys for inspiration. When we first moved to White House four years ago, I took Cayden to the park near our house and discovered that the playground there had nothing for him to do. Cayden couldn't even wheel around because the ground was covered with wood chips. I was so disappointed. I called the city, and they were very nice to me, understanding the situation. But there didn't seem to be any solution coming, so we just stopped going to that park.

Then the Miracle Recreation company heard about the boys and asked if Conner could help them renovate that very playground so that all kids in town could have fun there. Since many special-needs kids like Cayden can't speak for themselves, having a sibling describe what gives them joy was a smart idea. People from the company came to our house and spent hours asking Conner to describe what kids like his brother would enjoy.

Months later, when we attended the playground reopening, we found a lot of new equipment installed and things that Cayden could do. There was a merry-go-round with the seats scooped very deep so kids with trunk-control problems could ride without fear and without falling. Children without disabilities could have fun sinking deep in the buckets, too. Our favorite piece of new equipment was the swing, hanging at wheelchair level and built of trampoline material. That made it easy for a caregiver to place a child in the spongy cradle for a little spin. At the entrance to the playground stood a new sign that said, DEDICATED TO CONNER AND CAYDEN LONG.

So many blessings. So much love. That's not to say that life doesn't test us—we face new challenges and obstacles every single day, and heaven knows I create more than enough of my own bad luck. But my life has also been filled with so many small miracles. They haven't been the "When You Wish upon a Star" kind of miracles coming my way because I was so good and prayed so hard. But I now believe that miracles happen all the time—you just have to open your heart and mind to recognize and appreciate them.

Few of us start out in the best position to win the race. We all suffer defeats, sometimes a long string of them. But we also all have victories. Those small miracles are our moments of redemption. I see the miracle in that nook at the small of my mother's back where I fit perfectly and the fact that I was blessed to have such a happy, nurturing childhood with her. Certainly it's a miracle that a man like BJ Green could father a child like Conner. And I'll call it a miracle, and clearly a moment of redemption, when my father saved me from the clutches of my violent, drunken husband. It was also a miracle when Jeff and I decided—in unison and without a moment of thought—that no matter what, we would raise Cayden together. And it has definitely been a miracle that after Conner and Cayden started racing, I learned to drop the heavy weight of my shame.

Now, when we walk through the staging area before a race, I no longer worry what people will think if they know our whole story. That's why I'm sharing the whole story right here in this book. I know I may be judged harshly. And I know that I'm far from perfect. But I also have a message to share—it's a promise that my mom made to me, and my sons fulfilled. Everyone can find their miracle.

READERS
GROUP GUIDE

— discussion questions —

1. What were the pivotal moments in Jenny's childhood?
    How did these help or influence her later in life?

2. As a young girl, despite her mother's courageous effort to
    fight cancer, Jenny felt it was her responsibility to bring
    "light and life and hope" to her, and she admits it was a
    "heavy lift." How might each of these feelings have
    affected how Jenny went on to live her life?

3. After her mother's death, Jenny felt a certain survivor's
    strength and also permission to take some personal risks.
    How do you explain this response to the situation?

4. Living with her father was a challenge for Jenny, but he also proved to be—in some ways—a heroic figure in her life. How do you explain and rationalize the complexity of their relationship?

5. Jenny was strongly attracted to BJ Green in part because he was "dangerous." Why was this danger such a powerful draw for her? What is the appeal of the "bad boy" type, and why does it endure?

6. Jenny saw dropping out of school to work two jobs and move in spontaneously with a convict as a "romantic adventure." How do you explain that? What are the essential qualities of romance?

7. After BJ threatens and chokes Jenny, she can only think to call her father for help. Why? What in her experiences with him might have led her to believe he could—and would—help her?

8. Conner seemed to possess his impressive sensitivity, compassion and hopefulness from the very beginning. To what extent is this the result of natural temperament? What aspects of Jenny's personality and outlook might also have influenced him?

9. What did Jenny and Jeff find that they had in common during their slow, careful courtship? In what ways were they different? What is a healthy balance of similarities and differences in a marriage?

10. After the diagnosis of Cayden's cerebral palsy and the suggestion of institutional care, Jenny and Jeff powerfully declare that they are a family and that they will care for Cayden on their own. What were the positive outcomes of that decision? What were the sacrifices? Do you think the circumstances of her own childhood influenced Jenny in making her decision? If so, how?

11. From a very young age, Conner showed Cayden love, compassion and patience. Not all siblings share this strong a bond. How do you explain it? Do you think Cayden's condition played a role in drawing them closer?

12. In your opinion, what is the greatest influence on how siblings treat one another? Is it personality? Messages from parents? Societal examples?

13. Conner always seems to trust "seeing for himself," something many teens and adults struggle to do in the face of public opinion. What's the value of such independence of thought? Why is it difficult for so many?

14. Jenny admits to feeling shame for many things throughout her life. What causes shame? In what ways is that feeling social? Cultural? Personal? How do Conner and Cayden help their mother move beyond her shame?

15. Jenny believes in telling her boys the "straight truth," especially when it comes to her mistakes and difficulties. What does this mean? Why does she do it? How do you feel about exposing children to that level of honesty? Could you do it?

16. Conner seeks to play sports with his brother and doesn't quit until he can find a way. What's so valuable about participating in sports? What in particular do you think Conner wants to experience with his brother?

17. Despite being unable to express himself in words, Cayden clearly experiences joy when he races with his brother. What are the signs of this joy? What do you think Cayden likes most about the experience?

18. What is a miracle? How does the idea of "expecting" one differ from, say, "waiting" for one? How is this related to the family's philosophy of adapting to situations and "making things work"? Do you have a changed perspective on miracles after reading about the Long family?

19. Jenny says that it is the "small kindnesses ... that add up to love." What does she mean? How does this work?

20. A recurring theme in *Expect a Miracle* is how people look at others and make judgments based on their own opinions and beliefs. Judgments are frequently inconsistent—the Long family can receive "dirty looks" in a restaurant but cheers during a race. What are the flaws in how we judge others? If we were more thoughtful about how we evaluate people and their circumstances, do you think it would make the world a more positive place?

ACKNOWLEDGMENTS

THE FACT that this book exists at all is a miracle on its own. Jenny and Bob wish to thank a number of important people who have offered their skills and encouragement from the start of the process to the end.

FROM JENNY: A big thank-you to my awesome co-author Bob Der and the whole team of amazing people from Time Inc. who believed in me and supported our story. I also want to thank Jeff for being such a great dad to our boys. A big thank-you also to the Gildersleeve family, the LeBron James Family Foundation, our YMCA family, Miracle Recreation, and Courtney, Tonya, Susan, Vicki, Bonnie, Linda, Genevieve, Kayla and all the captains and angels across the world. And to anyone buying and reading this story, thank *you*.

FROM BOB: Respect and continued appreciation to the Long family—your story has already touched millions and hopefully will touch millions more. Special thanks to Roe D'Angelo and Danelle Morton for their expert guidance as our editors; the team at Time Inc. Books (past and present) for believing in the project and keeping it moving forward, including Stephen Koepp, Amy Lennard Goehner, Jonathan White, Joy Bomba, Michele Bove, Susan Hettleman and Jim Childs; the staff of

Sports Illustrated Kids, who first worked to present the story of Team Long Brothers in 2012, including Gary Gramling, Justin Tejada, Beth Bugler, Marguerite Schropp Lucarelli, Christina M. Tapper, Bob Schrumpf and Marilyn Goldman; the executives at *Sports Illustrated* and Time Inc. who have embraced the SportsKid of the Year program, including Paul Fichtenbaum, David Bauer, Christian Stone, Christine Rosa, Mark Ford and Ian Orefice; and the group at 10Ten Media for their support and good cheer, including Scott Gramling, Ian Knowles, Andrea Woo, Nina Pantic, Christian Rodriguez, Zach Cohen and Kaci Borowski. Thanks also to Dawn Kojak for the expert transcription. And, finally, great appreciation to the friends, co-workers and extended family who have made the journey more enjoyable and memorable over the years, including Paul DeGeorges, Neil Cohen, Craig Neff, Katherine and Charlie Newberger, Andrew McCloskey, Diane and Dan Bailey, and Dan Coleman.

ABOUT THE AUTHORS

JENNY LONG is the mother of Conner, 11, and Cayden, 9, who have competed in races together as Team Long Brothers since 2011. Jenny's youngest son, Cooper, is 5. Jenny is also president of My Team Triumph: Team Long Brothers of Middle Tennessee, an organization that seeks to spread to a wider audience the joy of racing with special-needs children.

BOB DER is managing director of 10Ten Media and the former managing editor and publisher of *Sports Illustrated Kids*. He lives in West Orange, New Jersey, with his wife Liz and sons James and Connor.

11-15